# Becoming a RURAL LAWYER

## From LawyerAvenue Press
# CAREER RESOURCES FOR A LIFE IN THE LAW

### The New What Can You Do With a Law Degree?
A Lawyer's Guide to Career Satisfaction Inside, Outside & Around the Law
By Larry Richard & Tanya Hanson • $30 / 220 pages (2012)

The New Lawyer Survival Guide, Vol. 1:
### From Lemons to Lemonade in the New Legal Job Market
Winning Job Search Strategies for Entry-Level Attorneys
By Richard L. Hermann • $30 / 254 pages (2012)

The New Lawyer Survival Guide, Vol. 2:
### Small Firms, Big Opportunity
How to Get Hired (and Succeed) in the New Legal Economy
By Linda Calvert Hanson, Samantha Williams • $30 /168 pages (2012)

The New Lawyer Survival Guide, Vol. 3:
### Becoming a Rural Lawyer
A Personal Guide to Establishing a Small Town Practice
By Bruce M. Cameron • $30 / 148 pages (2013)

### Solo by Choice 2011/2012 Edition
How to Be the Lawyer You Always Wanted to Be
By Carolyn Elefant • $45 / 306 pages (2nd Ed., 2011)

### Solo by Choice, The Companion Guide
34 Questions That Could Transform Your Legal Career
By Carolyn Elefant • $30 / 136 pages (2011)

### Should You Really Be a Lawyer?
The Guide to Smart Career Choices Before, During & After Law School
By Deborah Schneider & Gary Belsky • $25 / 276 pages (2nd Ed., 2013)

### How to Litigate
The Crash Course for Trial Counsel
By Martin L. Grayson • $30 / 170 pages (2013)

**Available at online bookstores**

The New Lawyer's
SURVIVAL GUIDE, VOL. 3

# Becoming a RURAL LAWYER

A Personal Guide to Establishing
a Small Town Practice

BRUCE M. CAMERON

DecisionBooks
SEATTLE, WASHINGTON

Published by LawyerAvenue Press and its imprint, DecisionBooks

Copyright c 2013. Bruce M. Cameron. All rights reserved.

Printed in the United States of America. No part of this book may be reproduced, stored in a retrieval system, or transmitted in any form or by any means, electronic, mechanical, photocopying, recording, or otherwise, without the prior written permission of Avenue Productions, Inc.

Cover design by Elizabeth Watson
Interior design by Rose Michelle Taverniti

Volume discounts available from LawyerAvenue Press.
Email to editor@LawyerAvenue.com, or write to Avenue Productions, 4701 SW Admiral Way #278, Seattle WA 98116

---

Library of Congress Cataloging-in-Publication Data

Cameron, Bruce M.
 Becoming a rural lawyer : a personal guide to establishing a small town practice / Bruce M. Cameron.
    pages cm
 ISBN 978-0-940675-75-9 (alk. paper)
1. Solo law practice--United States. 2. Practice of law--United States. 3. Law offices--United States. 4. Lawyers--United States. I. Title.
 KF300.C29 2013
 340.023'73--dc23
                        2013005760

# ACKNOWLEDGEMENTS

**A**s a solo attorney, you see your professional life waxing and waning according to your solitary efforts, often heedless of the fact that over there on the sidelines stand the unsung few (family, mentors, teachers, etc.) who provide the foundation that makes it possible for us to do what we do. To those who make up my support network, thank you. And while this book may have my name on the cover, it, too, came together through efforts of number of people, notably: my publisher, who spent a number of months convincing me to actually sit down and write this book, and for spending an equally long time whipping my ramblings into something that could be published; the rural lawyers I interviewed who generously gave of their time, helping me understand the "average" rural lawyer; and my wife who kindly acquiesces to be my unpaid assistant, editor, proofreader, and therapist. You all have my thanks. Any remaining errors in this book are due to my ineptitude. —BC

# TABLE OF CONTENTS

**I. PLANNING TO RELOCATE**  1
*Chapter 1*  Rural Practice: An Affair of the Heart  1
*Chapter 2*  Making it as a Rural Lawyer  4
*Chapter 3*  Where's My Starbucks?  11
*Chapter 4*  Not Enough Legal Work (and 7 Other Myths)  19
*Chapter 5*  Advice to Law Students & New Grads  22
*Chapter 6*  In Their Own Words  26

**II. MAKING THE MOVE**  31
*Chapter 7*  Finding a Place to Practice  31
*Chapter 8*  Life in a Small Town  36
*Chapter 9*  Meet a Few Small Town Lawyers  39
*Chapter 10*  My Own Rural Haven  41
*Chapter 11*  In Their Own Words  45

**III. A DAY IN THE LIFE**  49
*Chapter 12*  The Rural Client  49
*Chapter 13*  Fees & Consultations  53
*Chapter 14*  What Kinds of Cases  55
*Chapter 15*  Get Paid Up Front (and 10 Other Lessons)  58
*Chapter 16*  The Rural Jurist & Small Town Courts  63
*Chapter 17*  Marketing & Growing Your Rural Practice  66
*Chapter 18*  In Their Own Words  78

**IV. YOUR NEW LAW PRACTICE**  87
*Chapter 19*   Should You Buy a Practice?   87
*Chapter 20*   Hanging Your Shingle   92
*Chapter 21*   High-Tech in a Rural Setting   105
*Chapter 22*   In Their Own Words   112
*Chapter 23*   In Conclusion   115

**APPENDIX**   117
1   Q&A with Bruce Cameron   117
2   Outtakes from RuralLawyer.com   123
3   A New Practice Checklist   127
4   Bibliography   131
5   Print & Online Resources   133
6   Footnotes   136

# INTRODUCTION

*"This book owes its origins to a goat and a mid-life crisis."*

It would be nice to say I became a rural lawyer out of a noble desire to be of service to my community…or out of some detailed study of job market dynamics and economic trends. But it just wouldn't be true.

In fact, I never intended to live in a rural community. To a city boy like myself, country was just a place the Interstate ran through; a lot of tiny dots on a map where you filled the tank with overpriced unleaded, grabbed some coffee, and went on your way. Sure, I dreamed of having a summer cottage in New England someday.

But living rural 24/7? Not an option. And yet, in hindsight, my move to the country was inevitable.

You see, I married a country girl.

My wife is not one of those "boots-tight-jeans-knows-every-Patsy-Cline-song-by-heart" type of country girl, but a woman whose soul is truly drawn to quiet places at the edges of suburban civilization, and who finds beauty and peace in the wilderness. Of course, all the signs were there when we were dating. I would take her to movies, she would take me spelunking; I would take her RV camping, she would take me backpacking; I would take her to nice restaurants, she would feed me wild grub by the lake (deep-fried grasshoppers aren't all that bad).

After we got married, I thought about getting a pet; something conventional, like a drooling Labrador, a rescue cat, a parakeet. Instead, we got an unweaned baby goat. It was actually a housewarming gift for my sister-in-law, but she couldn't accept livestock. So, now the goat is living with us in a one bedroom house, and getting bigger with every meal. Space was at a premium. So, my wife and I went looking for a small farm that two graduate students can afford. Before long, we found a fixer-upper farmhouse with barn, tractor, and 25 wild acres. The goat is happy…and before long this city boy did find his country soul. Life in a farmhouse, a high tech job in the city. It was idyllic… for awhile.

After a few years, though, I was approaching the bottom of my Happiness Curve, and was in the middle of a full-blown midlife crisis. *What to do?* Get an Italian convertible? A mistress?

Or, maybe I should go to law school.

So, in 2004, I enrolled at Hamline University School of Law, a tier three private law school in Saint Paul, Minnesota.

My plan was to find an associate position with a firm doing IP work. After all, what firm wouldn't want an experienced software engineer/biomedical researcher-with-multiple-graduate-degrees-turned-lawyer? As it turns out, BigLaw wasn't ready for (or interested in) an over-40, second-career, "night school" lawyer (actually, I took all my classes on the weekends) who graduated from a tier-three school. What were my options? Well—given the approaching recession—the thought of going solo right out of law school, AND practicing in a small rural town, was the last thing I wanted to do. And yet as we all know, life is what happens while we're busy making other plans. Meanwhile, my rural neighbors kept reminding me of "ol' Bob Smith", now retired from his rural solo practice many years. And now and then, one of my neighbors would say to me, *"Y'know, we could use a lawyer around here. Maybe you should consider taking over ol' Bob's practice."*

So here I am. It's been some 26 years since a baby goat entered my life. And, against all my planning and expectations, I find myself engaged in a modestly successful solo law practice, renting an office on the edge of suburbia, and writing a book about why you should seriously consider starting a rural/small town practice of your own.

—Bruce M. Cameron, Esq.
March, 2013

# SECTION I. PLANNING TO RELOCATE

## CHAPTER 1

# Rural Law Practice: An Affair of the Heart

*"We've lived in Washington DC, Massachusetts, California, and enjoyed every place we've ever been. But our hearts remained in rural Minnesota. We like the quality of life here, and starting a rural law practice has [allowed] me to realize my dream of working in agriculture and with small town folks."*—Shawn Sween (class of 2004)

The decision to practice law in a rural area comes mostly from the heart. It has to.

Why else would one stray from the safe cultivation of marquee clients, and open a practice whose hallmark is one of general accessibility, where doors are open and walk-ins are welcome; where there are no power lunches, no schmoozing over cocktails, no marquee clients bringing in a steady stream of business. Just working people with their one-off matters and their expectations that the local lawyer will, to some degree, be involved in community service and community leadership. This is not pro bono service or networking; it is simple neighborliness, done more out of a spirit of giving than anything else. So, if you don't hear the call, if this is not as much a labor of love as it is just plain labor, you are going to have a hard time succeeding as a rural lawyer.

A rural legal practice is a type of practice that will have to come not only from your heart, but from your family's as well.

Like all rural enterprises, a rural practice is something of a family endeavor. And just as many a farmer is able to keep farming because a spouse has a "city" job, many a rural lawyer is able to meet their bills in a similar manner. Keep in mind that building a rural law practice is going to occupy 110 percent of your time and, if your daughters are freaking out because the nearest mall is half a county away, and your wife is upset because the only employment available is serving drinks to the grumpy old men at the local American Legion Post, and the aroma from the neighboring dairy farm has such an adhesive nature that it adversely impacts your teenager's dating opportunities, there will not be enough hours in the day to tend to your practice AND mollify your family.

## Do You Hear the Call?

We need more lawyers out here in the wilds of rural America.

But before you go trading in your Ferragamos for a set of gumboots, there are a few things you need to consider:

First, as the "new kid" in a small town, you have to adapt to the community and its ways. After all, they were there first, and, for the most part, they like things the way they are just fine. But don't worry, your new status should wear off in time, typically two to three generations (unless you do something so spectacular that everyone in the community takes notice. And if you do, it will earn you a nickname that in some way commemorates the event). Until then, you must get used to hearing your house referred to as the "Ol' Jones' Place", and you'll direct people to your office by telling them you've set up in the "Mercantile".

Second, rural living brings its own stresses and sensory annoyances. In small towns, a farmers "day" is long, typically from *can see to can't see* (i.e., from dawn to dark). As a consequence, the roar of a diesel tractor under load is pervasive, and it can carry for miles on a clear night. So, if you're already irritated at the sound of your neighbor's leaf-blower, then the drone of a tractor and the whine of a combine after midnight are sure to get under your skin. Let's talk about smells. Among the aromas unique to rural life are the metallic tang of herbicides/pesticides, the burnt musk of diesel exhaust, and the scent of a field redolent with fresh-spread manure on a summer afternoon. What about traffic? Well, the good news is that you can say goodbye to the urban gridlock that takes you 30 minutes to drive five miles. On the other hand, the experience of driving behind a tractor going 16 mph down a two-lane road is an exercise in patience.

Finally, keep in mind that life is not always cheaper in the country. There are some costs to a rural practice that cannot be easily deferred or avoided.

You must expect to put on more miles because the courts, law libraries, bar association meetings, and CLEs are further away. Office space tends to be a rare commodity, so expect to pay a premium for a quality location (the concept of shared-office suites and virtual offices have not yet reached rural America). In all likelihood, the only office space available will be former Main Street storefronts or older homes. So, expect to do some remodeling. Or, you might want to rent a room from the local bank, city hall, library, or work out of your home. As for phone communications, expect to pay a premium for cell and land-line service, as well as for a broadband connection (if it's available at all). The problem is that this country's biggest telecom providers have poor coverage in most rural areas, so you will be depending on a single, small, local provider.

Are all these costs worth it?

This former city boy thinks so, provided you go into it with your eyes wide open.

## CHAPTER 2

# Making it as a Rural Lawyer

*"What most city lawyers don't know is that lawyers in a small town are still looked at with respect, and we have a certain status. When you go to church, if the usher does not know you personally, he calls you 'counselor.' If he does know you, he calls you Steve* not *Mr. Harton. Furthermore, in a small town, even a lawyer with an ordinary practice can live in a nice house on the hill. It's [a] good life."* —STEVE HARTON

According to the US Census Bureau, "rural" is any place with fewer than 2,500 occupants located outside of a continuously built-up area with a population of 50,000 or more. So, a rural/small town lawyer would be an attorney working in a place with fewer than 2,500 occupants. The ABA's is broader in its definition, and considers "rural" any area with a population of less than 50,000. The ABA notes that the definition of "rural area" varies across the US. So, what might be rural in Vermont could well be a densely populated area in Alaska.

Thus the ABA's rural lawyer is one who works outside of a high-density population center. And there are at least four arguments for a rural/small town practice:

**Argument #1: Opportunity**. The rural bar is aging and, more often than not, law firms close when the last partner retires. For many small towns, the loss of a law firm means the loss of ready access to legal services and long drives to the next nearest attorney. Demographic data is starting to indicate that while young people, typically those of college age, tend to migrate away from rural areas, older people are migrating to rural areas. In fact, the so-called "retirement counties" in rural America are showing consistent growth as older adults exploit the perceived advantages of rural communities: a lower cost of living and a more relaxed lifestyle.[1] Businesses are also beginning to migrate to rural communities and for similar reasons, though businesses tend to relocate to the more *micropolitan*[2] areas where technology in the forms of reliable high-speed telecommunications and regular overnight shipping services is generally available. So, there you have it: the number one reason for considering practice in a rural area is…opportunity. Rural communities are seeing population growth, they are becoming more attractive to business, and at the same time they are losing access to legal services. Note: there are 490 potential clients per lawyer in New York (20.4 lawyers per 10,000 people, 19,306,183 people), and 2,272 potential clients per lawyer in North Dakota (4.4 lawyers per 10,000 people, 635,867 people).

☛ **The rural bar may be the last, truly under-exploited niche in the legal job market.**

*Argument #2: Status.* If you need an ego boost, being a lawyer in a small town is the way to go. Lawyers are the go-to guys when it comes to community problems. Don't want that power transmission line to go through the town? Need to know how to properly record your private cemetery? Have a problem writing a wind power ordinance? Talk to the local lawyer. It doesn't matter if he practices family law, he'll know what to do; the law's the law. It is great to feel needed, to have that recognition; something about being a big fish in a small pond. The downside is that you are actually expected to come up with answers even if they are outside of your field of practice.

☛ **It is great to feel needed, to have that recognition; something about being a big fish in a small pond.**

*Argument #3: Professional competition.* Among the rural bar, it is understood that competition is reserved for the court and not out in the community. Out of court, the rural bar is a relaxed casual beast; jeans and a sport coat is acceptable attire. In court, it is suit and tie so don't even think about leaving that three-piece suit and those Ferragamos back in the big city.

☛ **Out of court, the rural bar is a relaxed casual beast; jeans and a sport coat is acceptable attire.**

*Argument #4: Work-life balance.* Talking about work-life balance to most rural/small town folk is like talking about dialectical materialism to your goldfish. They'll listen politely, but don't really grasp the concept. Small towns are casual affairs and no one gets too upset if you occasionally hang a "gone fishing" sign on your door because it's understood there are times—be it a kid's ball practice, a friend's funeral, or simply time to de-stress (actually going fishing)—when one needs to rearrange the general pattern of their life. Kids are welcome in small towns and no one is surprised when your kids show up in your office. Many, if not most, businesses in a small town are family-run operations, and it is no surprise that where one finds parents, one will also find children. It is also a well-known fact that no child can outrun the small town grapevine. If your kid gets into mischief anywhere within eye-sight or ear-shot of an adult, it is quite likely that you will hear about it before the child gets home. It does not take long for folks to learn which child belongs to which parents.

> *"My small town is extremely family-friendly, and as the mother of four —including an infant—clients don't mind seeing them in my office when they stop by. In fact, my baby often sleeps in my lap while I work, and I have occasionally met drop-in clients while wearing the baby in a sling. While it certainly affects people's perceptions of me, I do not worry that it creates a negative image. Instead, I am happy to prove that lawyers can have a good quality-of-life, have a family, do a great job, and serve people's needs. On the other hand, there are fewer people here in town, so I need to make sure that I am marketing my practice appropriately. I can't count on a lot of foot traffic to bring in business. Also, when it comes to disputes between, it's extremely likely that I am going to personally know both parties."*—SHAWN SWEEN (CLASS OF 2004)

I found that I gained a sense of control over my life when I moved out of the metropolitan crush. Compared to the stress-inducing, Brownian motion of a freeway at 5:05 p.m., getting stuck behind a tractor moving glacially down a two-lane gravel road is positively relaxing, and it is quite liberating to give up the suburban ideal of mowing the lawn, washing the car, or installing holiday decorations in sync with one's neighbors. Reason enough for me to keep going rural.

☛ **Small towns are casual affairs and no one gets too upset if you occasionally hang a "gone fishing" sign on your door.**

### Is a Rural / Small Town Practice for You?

The typical image of the rural lawyer is that of a generalist. After all, it is rare to have more than one attorney set up shop in a small town, so the common expectation is that he/she will do everything, and typically there is the unspoken caveat that nothing will be done well. I believe the rural lawyer is more than just "location", and that he/she is an adaptive specialist rather than a generalist (regardless of the shingle that reads "… Law Firm, General Practice").

For example:

- Rural lawyers recognize that the needs of the community ebb and flow, and that there is a rhythm driving their practice.
- Rural lawyers manage the interconnectedness of practice areas while matching community need to relevant areas of law.
- Rural lawyers are entrepreneurial, continually adapting their practice. In hard times, they become knowledgeable in bankruptcy and divorce, recognizing that financial stress and marital strife are interconnected. In good times, the community's needs change; there are businesses to form and farms to expand. So, the rural lawyer adapts again, placing an emphasis on business law and real estate. And so it goes.

The rural lawyer is not market-driven, changing emphasis at every uptick or downturn of the stock market. As an adaptive specialist, the rural lawyer learns to takes a longer view, retooling only when the needs of the community have truly changed. To accomplish this, he or she must be a participant in his community, not just a mere observer. Also the rural bar is difficult to stereotype on matters of politics, race, sex, religion, etc. But one thing is guaranteed: you don't have to like greens and grits, drive a pickup, speak with a drawl, or even know the difference between a Holstein and a Hereford to practice in a rural community.

So, who are rural lawyers?

- They are attorneys willing to be entrepreneurs, and who either have—or are willing to develop—the ingenuity and drive to develop a practice that serves the needs of small business and private middle-class individuals.
- They tend to come to the practice by deliberate design. And, while family considerations and the attractions of rural living may play a role in the decision, the rural lawyer is looking for a career that offers autonomy AND is propelled by one's own enterprise rather than a career that is largely dependent on sponsorship for advancement and security.
- Rural lawyers often have something that binds them to the communities they serve. Generally they grew up in the area; perhaps not in the particular small town in which they practice, but within the same county. This last point is not there to scare off those of you who, like me, are coming to rural living and rural practice *de novo*. I mention it just to make

you aware that, during its initial stages, a rural practice is vulnerable, and it needs income to survive. To get that income, the rural practitioner needs to build ties to the community, and the process gets a jump-start if one is starting among family and friends rather than among strangers. Note: the hometown kid doesn't necessarily have a head start. Small towns have long memories, and stories (especially those of youthful indiscretions) only get better with age. So, while the rural transplant may have to build their community network from scratch, the home town kid is going to have to live with (and perhaps live down) the story of when they….

## The Entrepreneurial Lawyer

If you are going to practice law in a rural setting, you're going to have to be something of an entrepreneur. But don't worry, no one is born an entrepreneur. It's a learned skill. And if you made it through Civil Procedure in law school, you have all the necessary talents to be an entrepreneurial lawyer. In fact, an entrepreneurial legal career is nothing new; prior to the rise of the big metropolitan law firm it was the model for the legal profession. And while entrepreneurialism is currently out of favor with the metropolitan bar, it is still the career path of the rural solo or small firm lawyer.

Here's how it works:

The hallmark of the entrepreneurial rural lawyer is accessibility. Not the cultivation of marquee clients, but accessibility. That's so many rural lawyers have office on Main Street, with their doors open during business hours, and where walk-ins are expected. Think of a rural practice as a people-practice, because for most rural lawyers the majority of work is one-off legal problems of people living and working in the surrounding area. No power lunches or schmoozing over drinks to court marquee corporate clients. The rural lawyer builds his or her practice on the basis of community outreach.

The entrepreneurial rural lawyer is frequently also a political animal; most rural communities have the expectation that their local lawyers will, to some degree, be involved in community service and community leadership. In turn, these connections bring with them networking opportunities; the chance to interact with the people who form the town's core. These are the folks who know folks and their problems. They are the backbone of the rural grapevine. They are the rural lawyer's key relationships.

## The County Seat

Whether you call it the county seat, the parish seat, the borough seat or the shire town, this is the focal point of rural law. After all, where there are courthouses, there are lawyers.

County seats can be small towns or small cities; the fundamental difference is that small towns, regardless of their population, still have courthouses whereas small cities, in their hurry to morph into bedroom communities for some urbane metropolis, have justice centers. Justice centers are grand affairs, integrating glass, steel, and stone into monuments to bureaucratic judicial efficiency, providing one-stop shopping for all things legal, from the sheriff to the recorder, from the courtroom to the jail cell. They are places designed for those who assume that the efficiencies of consolidation and modernization make up for chronic underfunding. Here there is a cold sterility to the environment that seems to make courtesy appear artificial, and channels the mass of humanity that enters its walls into tired, well-worn roles.

On the other hand, courthouses are quiet buildings sitting in silent dignity on the edge of the town square; more cathedral than monument (while newer buildings housing the sheriff, the recorder and the jail, sit like handmaidens behind and to the side). Courthouses were built out of pride and are maintained out of tradition. There is warmth within those weathered walls, and the paneled, well-worn hallways and stairways encourage courtesy and seem to welcome all those who enter.

For the rural lawyer, the county seat holds a certain appeal; the convenient access to the courts, the economic vitality (relatively speaking), and the fact that the rural client base expects to find lawyers there, their offices nestled in the shadow of the courthouse. In some parts of this country, the county seat may also be the only significant population center in the county with ready access to health care, a broadband connection, and a varied shopping experience (they might even have a "big box" retailer). County seats are the first place lawyers head to and the last place lawyers leave, so the county seat may be the one place in rural America where it is possible to find a surfeit of lawyers. So before considering one particular county seat as your new home, count heads; if the person-to-lawyer ratio is less than about 500 to 1, you might want to consider looking in another county.

## Rural Practice is Evolving

There still seems to be some question whether a rural lawyer can have it all. I think you can, and by "all" I would include a quality practice, a sufficient income, *and* a good work-life practice.

But, like everything else in life, having it all comes with a price: the cost of relocation, the challenge of budgeting for student loans *and* start-up costs, and whether the rural community you select will have spousal employment opportunities. All things considered, the prospective rural lawyer does have many complex and difficult decisions ahead.

The good news is that rural communities are evolving, and rural law practice is evolving with them. You're no longer tied to the traditional billable hour and the full-service model. In fact, the successful rural lawyer these days realizes that somewhere between *pro-se* and full-service lies opportunity, and that whether you offer a half-hour contract review for $75 or limited scope engagement for $200 to help a couple complete the paperwork for their *pro-se* divorce, *there are fees to be made doing small things in small ways.*

Speaking of fees, the prospective rural lawyer needs to understand that the billable hour may not be the best way to attract clients or to collect fees. It's not that the billable hour is a bad method; it's just that the average rural client—whether they're in the "vanishing middle class" or among The One Percent—tends to be acutely aware of the value of a dollar, and they want to know in advance what a product or service may cost. For most of them, the concept of the billable hour and no fixed estimate of costs is just a lawyer's fancy way of asking for what amounts to a blank check. I'm not suggesting you abandon the billable hour and take up some alternative billing model; I'm suggesting that you adopt a fee-for-service model that includes firm estimates and some means of handling cost overruns (i.e., informing the client well in advance, and getting permission to continue or to withdraw if permission is denied, etc).

From my conversations with other rural lawyers, it seems that the key to successfully charging for one's services comes down to being flexible in one's billing model; taking from each method in moderation (say, charging for the hour, or the meeting, or the entire representation where appropriate). How much you charge is up to you. Just remember, the charges need to be reasonable and, of course, at the end of the month, what you take in needs to be greater than what you spent. Regardless of your billing model, the keys to successfully collecting your fees remain the same. You'll want to: (a) get at least some (all is preferable) of your fee up front, (b) bill promptly and regularly, and (c) accept credit cards.

If you're seriously considering living and working beyond the suburban sprawl, there are those who would have you prepare a backup plan; a Plan B to prepare for the eventuality of failure. My advice is just the opposite: *prepare for success*. If your business plan includes a *commitment* to your new community, you won't need an escape plan.

## CHAPTER 3

# Where's My Starbucks?

*"I grew up in the service business, and always liked working one-on-one with people. I never liked the hustle of the big city, though, and wanted a place to call home."*—BRUCE DORNER (CLASS OF 1977)

**R**elocation seems to be an American pastime.

Until 1900 (when the US government officially noted the passing of the Western frontier), America grew through an almost endless stream of settlers pushing west. Today, statistics indicate that one in five Americans change residences every year, though the migration tends to be more eastward and urban. Often we move, not for advancement, but out of a desire to find a better environment in which to start a business or raise a family. A 1995 Gallup poll indicated that 52 percent of the US population would like to live in a rural area and 29 percent would prefer to live in a city with a population of less than 100,000.[1] So, if you are thinking of packing your family up and heading out to some small, quiet town, it's normal (although you just may be swimming against the legal career stream).

*The only rule is that before you head out, have a plan.*

For starters, when you trade the big city life for a rural one, you are also trading that big city salary for a small town one. So, expect to make 25 percent less if your small town has a population in the 50,000 to 300,000 range, and 50 percent less if the population is under 50,000.[2]

For two-income families, that second job is another thing to consider.

If your spouse is unable to manage the commuter lifestyle, you're going to have to consider local employment (see *Where the Jobs Are…and Aren't* at the end of this chapter). Government jobs tend to be the most stable and secure, while those with the local "big" business run a close second (note: in a small town, the local school district is often the largest employer). Unfortunately these jobs usually go to those with connections in the local good ol' boy network (the smaller the town, the more this is true), or to those whose qualifications and interviewing skill make it readily apparent that you are head and shoulders more capable and competent than any of the local options.

### Housing: Think Outside the Box

Housing should be next on your list of considerations.

While rural places typically rank high in surveys looking at livability, the options for rural housing may be considered a step down from what is available in the big city. So, be prepared to think unconventionally. You may have to create your dream home yourself either by building new or investing sweat-equity into a "fixer-upper." You should note that what a rural realtor might see as a handyman special, you might see as one step removed from derelict. The first farm house my wife and I owned consisted of four exterior walls, two floors…and nothing else (no plumbing, no interior; nothing), and may once have been used to house livestock! A quaint place described to us as *just needing a bit of elbow grease*.

If you are thinking of renting, be aware that the rental availability is going to be dependent on population size and makeup.

Micropolitan areas, tourist destinations, and college towns are going to have a more robust rental market than their more dowdy cousins. And don't expect much from rural rentals outside of basic functionality. Expect them to be clean, maintained…and old. If you can find an apartment complex in your small town, expect few modern amenities; if you can find one with a pool count yourself lucky. If the town's telecom provider offers cable TV or Internet access, don't expect a connection in every room. Most likely your Internet signal will terminate in the room closest to where the phone lines enter the building.

If you have children, you are going to have to consider schools.

In most cases, there are three schooling options available in a small town: public schools, home schooling, and boarding schools (it is an unusual small town that has a local private K-12 schooling). Generally, small towns have good schools, and the thing that makes small town school districts work is parental and community involvement. Because schools are social centers (they are polling places, a source of live theater, and a source for live sporting events), there is a great deal of community interest in insuring schools stay open. PTA meetings and school open houses are standing-room-only affairs. While small town schools may not have as diverse a curriculum as their metropolitan counterparts, they do a good job with what they offer, so don't dismiss small town public schools out of hand, just do your due diligence first.

Finally, consider those other little amenities you and your family enjoy;

call it the Starbucks Question: can you live miles from the nearest Starbucks, Dominos, Krispy Kreme?

All but the smallest of small towns will have something in the way of public amenities: a local cafe, a bar (or three), a small restaurant, a park, a golf course, a bowling alley, a single screen cinema, or a library, but don't necessarily expect the big retail and food chains to be rushing out to rural America. Remember it is not all bad news and deprivation; there are gems to be found in small towns if you look for them. One of the largest manufacturer of handmade wooden toys is found in a small town[3], as are specialty art museums, artists, musicians, airports, gourmet restaurants, etc. Going rural does not mean deprivation, but there will be a little retooling of your expectations.

## Can You Afford to Relocate?

This is really one of those questions that only you can answer. You're the only one who knows what your financial circumstances are, and what it costs to run your family and to meet your financial goals. The bad news is that you will earn less in a small town, about 20 to 25 percent if you are looking at moving to a micropolitan area and up to 50 percent less if you are looking at a truly small town.[4] On the plus side, when you consider the cost of living, most studies show that it can be up to 30 percent cheaper to live in a small town.[5]

Now, just because eggs are cheaper in the country, don't expect everything else will be. In fact, perhaps surprisingly, you'll find that there will be little reduction in your food bill because you are either spending time and money traveling to the big city to find the foodstuffs you're used to, or you accept the limited selection and higher prices for the convenience of shopping locally. You should also expect to pay slightly more for utilities, and subscription TV (cable and satellite) can be much higher, too. On the other hand, over-the-air TV reception is still free and usually far better than similar reception in metro areas.

In most small towns, you'll find that what really lowers the cost of living is real estate. Your housing costs and real estate taxes are going to be lower than in the typical metropolitan area. And unless you are building new, you will find that rural property follows something like the real estate version of Moore's Law; you get twice the house at the same price, or the same house at half the price. The exceptions to this are college towns and tourist destinations; the demands there of a transient population are going to bring these costs back into the realm of the big city. The small town's lower housing prices often translates into lower costs for office space and lower prices for services from plumbers to lawyers.

You will find that sticker shock will come in two areas: transportation and telecommunications. Small towns are the heart and soul of American car culture and the two-car family is almost de rigueur. When you do get into the car to go somewhere that somewhere can be a 100-mile round-trip. Then there are the stealth costs of telephone and Internet. They appear to be the same or perhaps lower than those in the city, but not when you check the extent of the service provided against what you find in the city. In fact, when you compare apples-to-apples, the cost of rural telecommunications can easily be half again as much as what you might pay in suburbia.

### Married + Two Jobs

One reason lawyers may not be flocking to small towns is that a spouse or significant other (SO) may be reluctant to leave their career behind. Fair enough; jobs are tough to come by in this economy, and it is perfectly understandable that someone would prefer keeping a sure thing over packing off to the middle of nowhere…even if it is a particularly scenic middle-of-nowhere.

So if your spouse or SO is still talking to you after you first raised the idea of a rural practice, here are a few options:

**Commute.** Lots of folks commute to work. There are a couple of ways to work the commute thing. You can live in the small town and your SO can battle rush-hour traffic or stay in the city and you head out to your rural practice. The trick here is finding a small town that is close enough to the city to be a comfortable commute but not close enough to be a "bedroom" community. Folks that live in bedroom communities are too accustomed to traveling into town for their needs. So, setting up a practice here means that you would have to compete against the city lawyers for business. Living and working in a bedroom community is doable, but why add an additional layer of complexity to things.

**Telecommute.** Small towns are not, necessarily, the technological deserts they were a decade ago; broadband Internet, fiber optic voice lines, and overnight delivery are slowly penetrating rural America. So if your SO is one of the 50 million American workers eligible to telecommute, and you pick the right small town, perhaps telecommuting would open the door to your rural law career. In this case, the "right small town" is likely to be within a reasonable drive (say 90 minutes +/-) of a larger city, and will likely be close to a major road (I'd say major highway, but that phrase tends to bring to mind the Interstate highway system and not the sometimes two- sometimes four-lane highways that typically connect small towns to the rest of the world). This allows for the occasional commute into the city and increases the likelihood that there will be high-tech in this small town.

***Work outward.*** While it is more common for second-career lawyers than those starting their first, it is possible to develop a rural practice from a suburban office. I call it "practicing outward from the edge of suburbia". The advantages are that you attract both city clients and rural clients (and often the income from the city clients is what keeps the wolf at bay while you build the rural side of things), and you have a support system to fall back on (urban bars tend to be much more active than rural bars). The disadvantage of working from a suburban office is that you are competing with the city lawyers for city clients, you'll spend a lot of time on the road building and maintaining your rural referral networks, and (unless you are living in the small town), you'll have to deal with the fact you're not a local. And that can be a big deal. The average small town client considers lawyers to be fungible; the order of preference seems to be a) the local one, b) the one you know personally, c) the one a friend knows, d) the one someone you know refers you to… and e) all the rest.

## WHERE THE JOBS ARE (AND AREN'T)

Traditionally, rural lawyers are found in small firms and solo practices, in city and county government, on school boards and in school offices, and working for area hospitals and non-profits.

But given the realities of the current post-recession economics, an inexperienced lawyer's most likely path to a rural law career is as a solo practitioner, or as part of a small firm, or working for a county prosecutor or public defender (although these jobs are harder to find at a time of shrinking government budgets). Then again, you might find a position in the rural satellite office of some midsized law firm that wants to establish a regional presence. Please note: for some midsized firms, satellite offices do work well, but often last only for a few years before being closed for lack of profitability. For the lawyer who does find work in a satellite office, the key to success is to get involved in the community. Just like rural solos and small firm practitioners, you *must* commit to the small town, spend the majority of your working hours in the satellite office, and be willing to live where you work.

Are there alternatives? Yes.

The alternatives include teaching in colleges, working as in-house counsel for hospitals and other non-profit or not-for-profit entities. But these, too, are running up against shrinking budgets and the do-more-with-less realities of the current economic downturn. For example:

- As small rural hospitals are absorbed by larger, regional HMO's, the administrative and in-house counsel positions face consolidation. And these larger healthcare entities tend to look for in-house counsel with significant experience in health-care related law to fill their centralized and systemized departments, and most of these positions are filled by lateral hires rather than new law grads.

- Colleges tend to look for applicants with something more than simply a law degree. Generally, some teaching experience or a history of scholarly publication, and at least Master's, are what's required if your resume is to get a second look.
- As for rural non-profits and not-for-profit organizations, job openings tend to be rare, grant-funded, and of limited duration. Most of the organizations are short-staffed, but they tend to spend most of their budget on providing services rather than salaries. If you are looking for one of these positions, it helps if you have some fund-raising or grant-writing experience.

## MAKING THE MOVE

Law practice sales ads are now a fixture on Web sites such as Craigslist, for example. Many of these are aging small-town lawyers concerned about identifying and luring a competent replacement. To a much greater extent than in major cities, these rural practitioners are much more willing to mentor their putative successors during an overlap period and to introduce them around town, thanks to a love of and loyalty to their close-knit community. It is far easier today to undertake location research than it was back when this Wall Street lawyer performed his due diligence on possible rural practice locations in Upstate New York. Web sites like the Avery Index (*www.averyindex.com*) can tell you essential information like the per capita attorney population of each state. As this is being written, the big winners for the lowest numbers are:

| State | Number of Attorneys Per 10,000 Residents |
| --- | --- |
| North Dakota | 4.4 |
| Arkansas | 5.3 |
| South Dakota | 5.8 |
| Kansas | 5.8 |
| Idaho | 6.1 |
| Iowa | 6 |
| Wisconsin | 6.8 |
| New Mexico | 6.9 |
| Indiana | 6.9 |
| Kentucky | 7.1 |

These are extremely attractive statistics if you contemplate a rural relocation and practice. Especially when compared to the Big Legal Kahuna—the District of Columbia—with its 276.7 lawyers per 10,000 residents. In Washington, DC, you can throw a stick out of your office window and be certain that it will bounce off of at least five attorneys before it hits the pavement.

When you look at the Avery Index numbers, you need to be sufficiently sophisticated to note that the distribution of per capita attorneys is going to be highly uneven from one part of a state to another. What that means is that rural areas that are part of very heavily populated states may nevertheless be attractive practice locations. You can drive for hundreds of miles through parts of California, Texas, New York, Florida, Pennsylvania, Ohio, Illinois, Michigan, and New England that are so bereft of cities and masses of humanity that you think that you are in the Dakotas, Arkansas or Kansas.

The costs of entry into solo practice have plummeted everywhere, thanks to the technology revolution, and are even lower in rural areas. Computerized legal research options have relegated hard copy law libraries to the dustbin of history along with quill fountain pens and reading the law in lieu of attending law school. With competition to Westlaw and Lexis, legal research is becoming less expensive at the same time that it is becoming more expansive. Word processing software means that you really do not need a secretary, certainly not when you are in an initial launch phase of your practice. Voicemail can serve as a bargain basement receptionist. A home office is an easy thing to establish and can serve you ably until you begin to generate cash flow. Moreover, zoning restrictions are much looser in rural America.

Alternatively, if you feel that an office is essential from the outset, rent is generally cheap, far less expensive than in urban areas.

I know an attorney in a rural locale who rents 3,000 square feet of space above the local bank (a great location for referral business from the first floor) for—are you ready for this?—$125 per month! His landlord has not raised his rent in this century. In contrast, 3,000 square feet in downtown Washington, DC is now going for more than $12,000 per month with an annual 3.5 percent escalator and real estate tax pass-through! This attorney's offices are as nicely appointed as any partner's office in a large law firm.

Marketing your practice in a small community is also easier and cheaper.

Rotary, Kiwanis, Elks, Moose and Lions clubs abound, and are always eager for new members and for speakers on topical matters. Local newspapers are often keen for new arrivals to interview and may even accord you op-ed page space in print and online for a legal advice column. Local bar associations are excellent referral agencies. Becoming active in the community can also pay off handsomely.

In summary, there is a lot to recommend to attorneys seeking something different from the conventional career route. America is full of small ponds conducive to the arrival of big and small legal fish.

By Richard L. Hermann, Esq., Author, *From Lemons to Lemonade in the New Legal Job Market* (2012)

---

**Visit the author's Website at**
**www.RURALLAWYER.com**

---

## CHAPTER 4

# Not Enough Legal Work (and 7 Other Myths)

*"It's a misconception that* [small town lawyers] *can't handle substantial, complex matters. After making partner* [in Atlanta], *I decided to leave the big city, and I'm as good a lawyer now as I would be had I remained."*
—Mark Cobb (class of 1991)

Perhaps the biggest myth about small towns is that they aren't places of refinement and culture. In fact, often the opposite is true, because the arts, music, theater, and dance have NOT forsaken small towns, and folks in small towns have been culturally exposed overseas as part of their military service or their education. And while small town business people may not be Wall Street deal-makers, the average farmer runs a million dollar-plus enterprise. What follows are a few more common misconceptions about the rural bar that should be put to rest.

***Myth #1: There is not enough work out there.*** While it may not be raining soup, there is plenty of work for rural/small town lawyers. In fact, the little known secret about rural lawyering is that the need for legal services remains constant over time even as the supply of lawyers is diminishing (note: only 20 percent of practicing lawyers live and practice in towns with populations of 50,000 or less). The thing to keep in mind, though, is that to succeed a rural lawyer must first earn the trust and confidence of the community. Don't expect your reputation to precede you; most small towns are not going to be all that impressed by past triumphs, law school accolades, or that you went to a Tier 1 school. In fact, too much self-promotion will cause small town folks to avoid you (note: pomposity breeds skepticism; small towns figure no one is *that* good). In a small community, you have to be seen as accessible and competent, and you have to be a person first and a lawyer second. If you can achieve that balance, the work will come.

***Myth #2: I can't afford to work at a lower rate***. There's no doubt that rural lawyers have lower rates then their urban counterparts. But before dismissing a rural practice out of hand (either because it doesn't generate a big city salary, or you carry a heavy law school debt load), remember that small towns lack the big city cost-of-living. For example, the average lawyer in California will earn approximately $88,000/year while the average lawyer in Montana earns around $48,000 (based on 2007 US Census data). Yet if you adjust for cost of living, that $48,000 has the same purchasing power in Montana as $101,000 in California! Now, this is in no way a scientific comparison. It simply illustrates that you should not dismiss the idea of a rural practice because your gross salary would be less than in a big city. Do the math, and you may find that you'll have greater earning power in a small town.

***Myth #3: I'd feel isolated.*** Well, yes, if you're a solo practitioner in a small town, you are going to be alone; just you, perhaps your staff, and whoever happens to drop by. But thanks to Twitter, LinkedIn, Facebook, legal listservs, and the entire social networking revolution, the small town practitioner is no longer isolated from the rest of the legal community. Then, again, the rural lawyer has never really ever practiced in isolation. Rural lawyers have always built loose webs of social, civic, and legal networks because the one constant truth is that small towns tend to hire "their own" before they hire outsiders, and there are really only two ways to become one of their own: (a) arrange matters so that your family has lived in the town for at least three generations, or (b) be a "joiner". Small towns appreciate those who volunteer.

***Myth #4: I'd miss out on challenging legal work.*** Yes, the rural lawyer does miss out on things like M&A, intellectual property, securitization, and international corporate tax law. But if you're honest about it, the average metropolitan lawyer misses out on those things, too. Perhaps the key word here is "challenge". You'll find the average rural lawyer doing those small, messy—but challenging—legal things that matter to people. Things like family law, estate planning, civil and criminal defense, mechanics liens and construction matters, personal injury, bankruptcies, small business transactions, real estate, debt collection, agriculture law, and municipal law. And the average rural lawyer practices within a legal community that emphasizes and fosters collegiality and respect rather than one that seems to reward incivility and competition. See the end of Chapter 14 (*A Peek into My Crystal Ball*) for what are becoming the hot areas of rural practice.

***Myth #5: I wouldn't be exposed to a variety of practice areas***. If you mean that you won't be exposed to a fixed schedule of well-defined rotations through the various departments of a major law firm, you are absolutely right. But rural lawyers have to be a bit more flexible, and be able to write a Will, open a probate, handle a residential real estate closing, serve a summons and complaint in a divorce action, and defend a DUI case. And that's just what's on the agenda for Monday.

***Myth #6: I'd miss out on the Biglaw experience***. There is no denying that a rural practice, even one in a small firm, is not going to offer the same slow, steady climb toward success that a big metropolitan firm offers. Since the rural lawyer has to be ready for direct client interaction and courtroom appearances from Day 1, rural practice is more like jumping directly into the deep end of the pool. Look, rural practice is not for everyone, nor is a career in Biglaw. You have to listen to your muse. If your dream is to build a practice in international mergers and acquisitions, and you require the diversity and density of metropolitan life, then you'll never be happy in small town USA.

***Myth #7: Rural lawyers aren't as good or as sophisticated as big city lawyers.*** Don't underestimate the small town lawyer. The lawyer opening his or her storefront office on Monday morning is just as likely to be a Harvard Law grad (Order of the Coif, magna cum laude) as a graduate of a Tier 4 law school. Small towns are not big on credentials; they value competence over accolades. And the rural lawyer soon learns that advertising your professional expertise and legal acumen is an exercise in futility, simply because no one cares. So under that meek, mild-mannered disguise, a rural lawyer may be a top-notch litigator, an expert in estate planning, or a real estate wizard. Rural lawyers are not practicing out in the sticks because they aren't talented; they practice there because they choose to.

***Myth #8: Rural law is all back-room deals between the good ol' boys.*** Hate to bust this myth, but the notion that rural law is what's cooked up between an aging, semi-senile judge and a couple of conniving, good ol' country lawyers is "Hollywood" not reality. The reality is that the rural bar—from the knowledgeable and keenly acute jurists to the talented lawyers—is sophisticated, technologically savvy…and welcoming. Rural courts may have their local customs (like preferring blue ink for signatures, or three-inch top margins on any order that might be recorded in a land abstract, or holding foreclosure sales on the courthouse steps), but these are idiosyncrasies that can be easily found out by asking the court clerk. For details, see Chapter 16.

## CHAPTER 5

# Advice to Law Students & New Grads

*"It wasn't so much the legal skills* [for which I was unprepared], *but rather the skills necessary to run a business. I found I knew how to practice, but running my own business was an eye-opener and required me to learn a whole new skill-set."*—John Thrasher (class of 1993)

**B**ased on conversations with rural lawyers around the country, I've concluded that each rural lawyer's career is unique—to that lawyer and to the community they serve—and that there is no one way or single resource that will prepare you for a career as a rural lawyer. What I can offer are some general observations intertwined with a smattering of "if I were to do it over again."

***Notes to a 1L***. If I were a 1L considering a career as a rural solo, and I had enough of a handle on the whole law school experience to have any reserve brain power to contemplate such things, I would start by trying to gaining some understanding of how to manage a business. For any small town or rural practice, you are going to spend almost as much time managing the business of a law practice as you are on the actual practice of law. While there are a number of fine books out there that cover going solo from the lawyer's perspective (for example, Carolyn Elefant's *Solo by Choice* and Jay Foonberg's *How to Start and Build a Law Practice*), what you really want at this stage is to learn about the ins and outs of running and marketing a business. So, get in touch with the Service Corps of Retired Executives (SCORE), an arm of the federal Small Business Administration. SCORE offers mentoring, webinars, newsletters, online guides and live classes, all designed to help you start and grow a business. All these resources are provided at little to no cost by SCORE volunteers (working or retired business owners, executives and corporate leaders). Getting a SCORE mentor now means one less networking connection you have to make during the crazy hectic early days of your practice; plus you have three years to figure out the business side of things.

As for preparing for the lawyering part, look to those parts of the law that interest you and direct your studies in those areas. The rural lawyer, once the epitome of the general practitioner, is now becoming much more of a specialist, though it may be a general sort of specialization where probate work leads to estate planning which in turn leads to real estate work which leads back to probate work. For those rural attorneys with an interest in criminal law, it is quite common to find them spending the early years of their practice working for a county prosecutor's office or clerking for a county judge. So, now is the time to:

- Start thinking about which small town/towns you'd like to practice in. Knowing where you want to practice can often influence your decisions on the type of law you want to practice. Think "niche"; your small town may not be able to support another criminal lawyer, but it sure could use a family practitioner. Look before you leap.
- Start building contacts within the business and legal communities of "your small town". These are going to be your referral sources and possible mentors. Get an idea how your small town works and how you can fit in with the business community.
- See what internship opportunities are available. Don't limit this search to your small town; see what is available in similar communities in the area. Check with the county judges. Could any of them use a volunteer clerk for a month or so? How about the county prosecutor? How about the county legal aid? Yes, paid work is preferable, but in these days of vastly reduced budgets and strained court resources, play the long game; being a willing volunteer may open far more doors and get you far more opportunities later.

**Notes to a 2L.** At this point, you need to ask yourself: do you want to be a rural solo, or are you simply looking for a legal career with a small firm in a small town? If the latter, remember these are not jobs you are going to find via OCI; these are the kinds of jobs you find through a friend of a friend of a friend or discover through a one-line classified ad on a state bar's Web site. These are also the kinds of jobs that will expect you to be somewhat productive from day one so you may want to start volunteering at your local legal aid office or law school clinic.

It is possible to go solo right out of school. Just be prepared. Go in with your eyes wide open and **have a plan**. Now is the time to start reading those "how to be a solo lawyer" books and start roughing out a business plan for your practice. Nothing too complex (generalities are quite acceptable), but you should start thinking about how you are going to finance this venture, the contacts you should be making, and the goals you'd like to reach.

In either case, now is also the time to start thinking about and looking for your small town. If you decide to go the small firm route (get a copy of *Small Firms, Big Opportunity*), your town is going to come with the job. But if you are going to go solo, you have a bit more choice and should spend a little time thinking about where you might want to practice. Generally solos tend to return to the vicinity of their home town or pick a region that attracts them. But in these times of a declining rural bar, it may be worth your while to do a little research and see if there are any state bar association initiatives (like South Dakota's Project Rural Practice) aimed at repopulating the rural bar. At best, these programs may be able to help provide resources to fledgling rural lawyers; if nothing else they may be able to help you identify potential markets and connect you with retiring lawyers.

**Notes to a 3L**. There is little doubt that the new attorney knows a significant amount of legal knowledge. But the ability to apply it to practical situations is a real challenge. Spend time sitting at the courthouse in your small town to see how cases actually move. Ask an attorney if you can sit in on a client intake unless you've had experience in these matters. Above all, ask questions!

## Jumping into the Deep End of the Pool

So, you're seriously thinking of solo'ing right of school. Great! Here are some things to keep in mind:

If you can pass the bar exam, you are (or at least your State Bar thinks you are) competent to practice law. Period, end of discussion. So never doubt that you are sufficiently prepared to go out there and commit random acts of lawyerism. That nagging doubt, that fear that sneaks up in the quiet hours of the night, does not feed on your lack of competence; it feeds on your lack of experience. The good news is that there's a cure for that…time. If you need to gain experience, try asking other lawyers for overflow work, look for *pro bono* opportunities, or seek out court-appointed work. It may not pay much (if it pays at all), but it will get you experience and provide contacts that can help you build your client base. The key here is to be focused.

To further ease those nagging doubts, keep three phone numbers on your speed dial: the number of your state's ethics board, the number of your state's Lawyers Concerned for Lawyers group, and the number of a colleague/

mentor (or join the ABA's *SoloSez* listserv; with 3000+ members, it's both a discussion group and a support group). Call your board of professional responsibility if you have even the slightest doubt about the ethics of what you are about to do. During the early days of your practice, it is cheaper to be overly prudent (phone calls are free, an ethics complaint isn't) even if you did ace your PR class. Most state bar associations have a Lawyers Concerned For Lawyers (or similar named group) to help with the various stresses faced by lawyers and their families. These are good people, lawyers all, who've been there and done that, and they can help even if all you need is someone with whom to have a cup of coffee. The time to call them is when you think that perhaps, maybe, things might be getting a bit out of hand (the sooner you call them, the sooner your life can get back to normal). Finally, you need to have a colleague or colleagues from whom you can get a reality check, someone you can count on to give you a straight answer to the question: *"Is it me or is this client insane?"*

**Visit the author's Website at
www.RURALLAWYER.com**

# CHAPTER 6

# In Their Own Words

### Q: Why did you establish a small town practice?

*"I grew up in the service business, and always liked working one-on-one with people. I never liked the hustle of the big city and wanted a place to call home."*
—Bruce Dorner (class of 1977)

*"I graduated from this town, and decided to come back [to practice law]. I wanted to have my kids close to my parents and brothers, and learn why I love the land and farming."*—Pat Dillon (class of 2003)

*"My wife and I are from Atlanta. We chose a small town* [in Georgia] *because of the quality of life, the ability to participate in causes we support, and we wanted support in our lives and in the rearing of our children. We chose to live near downtown, and we're able to walk to the post office, the bank, several restaurants, the local museum, church, and to several friends' houses. We see and interact with people every day and relationships are built."*
—Mark Cobb (class of 1991)

*"After four years of a 200-mile daily commute, I wanted to regain control of my life. Establishing a practice in my home has allowed me to do just that. And although I practice in a small town, my practice is not confined to it."*
—Karen Holman (class of 2009)

*"I wanted to live in a small town to provide my four small children the security, space and community that small towns offer. Working [here] helps keep my overhead low, and [with] technology, my client base extends way past the limits of my small village. I'm active in community improvement and economic development, so when I graduated from my Master's program and decided to*

*open my own law office, I knew I had to 'practice what I preach' by keeping my business in town and investing in my own community."*
—Mindy Rush Chipman (class of 2077)

"We've lived in Washington DC, Massachusetts, and California, and enjoyed every place we've ever been. But our hearts remained in rural Minnesota. My husband and I grew up in this small town, and both sets of our parents [still] live here. More generally, however, we like the quality of life in rural communities, and starting a rural law practice has [allowed] *me to realize my dream of working in agriculture and with small town folks. [Now, when we] go to the store, the post office, the bank, and other local businesses, we greet the owners by name, and discuss local events.* [In my experience,], *the people in small towns are sophisticated. They run businesses, form contracts, sell real estate, conduct estate planning, and all the other legal work that happens in cities as well. I've found a real need for access to legal services in this and surrounding small towns* [without my clients] *having to travel 20–45 minutes to meet with an attorney."*—Shawn Sween (class of 2004)

"[I started a small town practice] *to have the flexibility to keep my own schedule and to provide a quality of life where my kids get to spend time being kids without worrying about them. Also,* [I wanted to make] *a positive difference in our neighbors' lives and in the community."*
—John Thrasher (class of 1993)

## Q: Can you open a rural practice straight from law school?

"Yes, that's what I did. But it takes *a lot of work and a couple years with almost no income."*—Fred Peet (class of 1993)

"A small town isn't for you if you prefer three-piece suits and depositions in plush conference rooms, and want the support of a team in a large office. But if you're a self-starter who wants to get your hands dirty—and make your own coffee—[a small town practice] *is a great way to go."*
—Bruce Dorner (class of 1977)

"Perhaps with family or very close friends in the area it might be possible. [Opening a rural practice straight from law school] *takes someone willing to throw themselves into the community: church, nonprofits, local boards, etc. Also, when I first looked into moving into the town in which I now live, a resident lawyer advised me not to move here until I was married. There are few marriage prospects [he said], and single life is boring.* [At the time] *that infuriated me, but now that I am married and living here, I understand the wisdom of* [his] *statement."*—MARK COBB (CLASS OF 1991)

"[If you're just starting out], *you have to be willing to do the dirty work that established lawyers don't want. Like taking criminal appointments, mental health cases, juvenile court appointments, or probating a local case where the decedent dies with some property but not enough to justify a giant fee,* [Opening a rural practice straight from law school] *is doable with work and personal relationships. But it would be easier to get into practice in an area you are from than coming cold turkey to a new area."*—PAT DILLON (CLASS OF 2003)

*"Many law schools do not teach students the actual practical business of practicing law.* [So], *the biggest obstacle to being a* [small town] *solo straight out of law school is* [that locals will wonder] *if you can actually do the work. The new lawyer will need to have the confidence and tenacity to learn the practice of law. It's certainly not a challenge just anyone can undertake, but I do believe it is possible for a person with the right attitude and work ethic."*
—SHAWN SWEEN (CLASS OF 2004)

## Q: How do you break into the rural bar?

*"Taking court appointments is a great way to familiarize yourself with the judges and court personnel, and the procedures."*
—MINDY RUSH CHIPMAN (CLASS OF 2007)

*"Stick your hand out, say hello and ask questions."*
—BRUCE DORNER (CLASS OF 1977)

*"Drink with the other lawyers."*—MARK COBB (CLASS OF 1991)

*"Find a mentor, or at least talk to a few practitioners and* [get] *the lay of the land so that you can adapt to the market you're in."*
—JOHN THRASHER (CLASS OF 1993)

"[In a small town], *you need to establish a reputation as a straight-shooter; fancy suits, shoes, and shiny foreign cars will not endear you to the population. You need to be credible when you go to the co-op to buy feed, even if it is only for your kid's 4-H rabbit."*—PAT DILLON (CLASS OF 2003)

*"Keep telling everyone you know that you have opened your office."*
—Fred Peet (class of 1993)

## Q: What are some of the misconceptions about the rural bar?

*"It's a misconception that* [we practice in a small town] *because we couldn't go where we wanted to. The truth is, we're here because we want to be here."*
—Karen Holman (class of 2009)

*"It's a misconception that* [all small town lawyers] *play golf and make back room deals with other lawyers that are based on the good ol' boy system."*
—Pat Dillon (class of 2003)

*"It's a misconception that* [small town lawyers] *cannot handle substantial, complex matters. After making partner* [in Atlanta], *I decided to leave, and I'm as good a lawyer now as I would be* [had I remained] *in a big city."*
—Mark Cobb (class of 1991)

## Q: What are some of the characteristics of the rural bar?

*"When my local district judge swore me in, he personally got me a cup of coffee and took me around to all the court personnel for introductions. Everyone was so welcoming and excited that there was going to be someone new to take on some court-appointed work in juvenile court."*
—Mindy Rush Chipman (class of 2007)

*"I have clients come in wearing chore boots, covered in grain dust, or coming directly from morning mass. They don't always make appointments, and they expect you to be able to answer questions in the grocery store, in the line at the grain elevator line, or at a local sporting event. I have been paid in LP tanks, tractors, pans of brownies, and tractor weights. I have driven a combine and a tractor, wearing clothes I wore to court in the morning."*
—Pat Dillon (class of 2003)

*"*[I] *can spend* [more] *time with my family. For example, when my kids get out of school at 11:30 on Fridays, I can take them skiing in the winter."*
—John Thrasher (class of 1993)

*"If you are coming back to* [your own] *small town, you probably would have enough name-recognition. But without any connection to the area it would be very hard. Most frugal and tight-lipped Yankees would not go to a new attorney*

*to start talking about their problems and how to resolve them. They would rather go to an attorney who they know."*—John Thrasher (class of 1993)

## Q: What are the pros and cons of rural practice?

*"The biggest pro is that I know everyone in town, and the biggest con is that I know everyone in town. It's tough when you're asked to represent a party in a case where you are neighbors with them both."*
—Mindy Rush Chipman (class of 2007)

*"[On the one hand], I was the only business owner under age 35 to be asked to be on the rural development board, the hospital fund raising focus group, and other community based organizations. Because of my status as a lawyer, I gain instant access to the town's decision-makers and leaders, and if I want a loan I can call the local banks and get hold of the presidents if I wanted to. [On the other hand], if my computers go down, the computer repair guy is a 30-minute drive away so it can take as much as three days to get my computers up and running again."*—Pat Dillon (class of 2003)

*"[Rural practice comes with several pros and cons]. On the one hand, I can meet clients in jeans and sneakers. It often puts people at ease to see that I am a regular person, too. My small town is extremely family-friendly, and as the mother of four—including an infant—clients don't mind seeing them in my office when they stop by. In fact, my baby often sleeps in my lap while I work, and I have occasionally met drop-in clients while wearing the baby in a sling. While it certainly affects people's perceptions of me, I do not worry that it creates a negative image. Instead, I am happy to prove that lawyers can have a good quality-of-life, have a family, do a great job, and serve people's needs. On the other hand, there are fewer people here in town, so I need to make sure that I am marketing my practice appropriately. I can't count on a lot of foot traffic to bring in business. Also, when it comes to disputes between, it's extremely likely that I am going to personally know both parties."*
—Shawn Sween (class of 2004)

# SECTION II. MAKING THE MOVE

## CHAPTER 7

## Finding a Place to Practice

*"An attorney should choose a small town to which he* [or she] *has ties already. If not, look for a community with a vibrant business community."*
—Shawn Sween (class of 2004)

Between Maine and California there are some 128,000 towns with populations of 25,000 or less, according to the US Census Bureau.

Finding your ideal place to practice will be a personal journey.

There are countless "find-your-ideal-community" books, magazines, and online resources to help localize your search (see Appendices 4 and 5). Ultimately, you will need to make the final search on your own, actually walking the streets and breathing the air of the small towns under consideration. **Author note:** *the ideal place to practice law will be where your concept of the ideal small town intersects with your notion of the ideal client; where your vision of how you'd like to practice law is complemented by the expectations of the client base.*

As you'll discover, every small town has a distinct, immutable style, so you will need to "try on" a few before making your decision. And the more detailed your vision, the easier it will be to isolate one community from thousands. It takes time to find the town that suits you; the one that feels like home. Naturally, if you have never lived in a small town, spending a few long weekends in them will help to ease the culture shock.

In my case, becoming a rural lawyer was more happenstance than planning. I just happened to be living in a rural area when law school ended, and I decided to go solo. And, of course, there were those goats I mentioned in the Introduction to this book. So, don't do what I did; it's like playing musical chairs with your law career, building on what presents itself when the music stops. If you're smart, you'll find a small town the right way. And the right way requires deliberation; it takes time to define what you want, what are your must-have amenities, and which of those you can't live without.

Here are just a few considerations:

- What is your preferred climate?
- How big a town do you want?
- What level of taxation can you live with?
- What are you prepared to spend for housing?
- What do you want from the area's educational system?
- How important is ready access to an airport?
- What recreational activities are necessary?
- Are museums, symphonies, theaters, opera, or dance troupes necessary parts of your life?
- What about professional sporting events?

Before committing to a town, I suggest you subscribe to the local newspaper to get a sense of the big issues facing the town, and how things are handled. If you can, spend several long weekends in the community…and not just during the most pleasant season. For example, here in Minnesota you can easily fall in love with its small towns in autumn, when the air is crisp, the sky is clear, and the apples are ripe. You would have an entirely different opinion, though, when the winter snow can reach your waist, and the daytime temperatures can be so low that spit freezes before it hits the ground.

Use your familiarization trips to ask yourself, "*Can I live here and be a part of this community*"? When you visit, avoid the touristy stuff, and really get to know the community. For example:

- Talk to the folks at the local Chamber of Commerce, and get a sense of the business community.
- Attend a town council meeting, and talk to council members afterward. Get a sense of the town's general health and well-being.
- Tour the local high school if possible.
- If you normally attend religious services, attend one in the small town. If the local services don't meet your needs, but there is a suitable service nearby, take a drive and attend that. Would you be willing to make that drive regularly?
- Go to real estate open houses and get a feel for the local housing market.
- If you are considering moving to a county seat, sit through a court session or two and see how the court works.
- If there's another lawyer in town, see if you can meet him or her for coffee (or lunch). Ask about their practice and their opinions of the local courts and the town itself.

- Check out the local grocery. Does it carry all the items on your basic weekly shopping list?
- Take a drive through the town; wander around a bit. Is this a place you could feel at home?

---

*To help you narrow your selection, here are eight categories to ponder:*

## THE CLIMATE

You prefer summer to be: hot, humid, moderate, dry, or cool

You prefer winter to be: cold, snowy, temperate, or warm?

You prefer autumn to be: short and sweet, or long, lingering and full of color?

You prefer spring to be: rainy and green, or a quick interlude before summer?

## THE ENVIRONMENT

You prefer to be on the coast, in the mountains, on the prairie, down by the river/stream/lake, or surrounded by desert.

## THE LOCAL ECONOMY

You would rather have low sales taxes, low income taxes, or low property taxes (in this economy, don't be surprised if you can only find the first or the third)

You prefer a region where the overall unemployment rate is low, or there is high job growth, or the overall cost of living is low

You prefer a region where the median cost of a house is low, or its homes are appreciating in value?

## THE TRANSPORTATION OPTIONS

Do you need an airport nearby? Does it have to support commercial air travel, or would general aviation meet your needs?

## THE HEALTH CARE OPTIONS

Close proximity to a hospital, or to a teaching hospital?

Low average costs?

Low patient-to-doctor ratios?

## THE EDUCATIONAL OPTIONS

Are you looking for a town with private schools, or will public education do?

Does there have to be a high graduation rate, low dropout rate, low pupil to teacher ratio, or better than average per pupil spending?

Does there need to be a college or university in the vicinity?

Does it have to be a top-rated school?

Does the town's population need to be highly educated?

What amenities do you want to find in your small town?

**OUTDOOR SPORTS**

Close proximity to professional or collegiate sports?

Availability of adult or youth amateur sports leagues?

Opportunities for hunting or fishing?

**ARTS, SCIENCE & CULTURE**

Should there be art galleries in the area?

Do you need professional theater, or will the local cinema and an amateur drama society do?

Can you live without the opera or ballet? Is the symphony a must?

Is a large public library a requirement, or could live with a small one that has an inter-library loan program?

Do you need to be close to museums, zoos, or aquariums?

Do you need a Starbucks on every other corner?

---

### And my personal suggestions...

***Look for a town with a traditional downtown, a high school, and a hospital.*** These are signs of a vigorous community, and a population large enough to support a law firm. Education and health care are people-magnets; a community that can provide these necessities has growth potential and is more likely to retain its young couples and new families. If you have to choose between a town with a high school and one with hospital, choose the one with the school. High schools are community-gathering places and are a focal point for a small town's social life. Watch out for small towns that lack a traditional downtown. If all the businesses are concentrated in strip malls, you may be looking at a bedroom community on the edge of suburbia. Likewise, be wary of small towns whose downtown is mostly shuttered. This is a sign of a town that is failing economically.

***Look for a town successfully managing its social & economic aspirations.*** Small towns desire to remain small socially, but economically the town desires to become large. Every small town approaches this balance differently; some seem to rely on the power of social clubs and volunteer organizations to maintain a sense of community and to balance the political rush towards economic development. Others temper growth using the power of bureaucratic inertia to insure that when growth occurs it has minimal impact on the social and physical character of the town. Be wary of the extremes. Small towns that seem to be doubling down and going all in on "billion dollar" economic development schemes are gambling with your future taxes, those on the other end of the spectrum are stagnating.

**Look for a town with an active Chamber of Commerce and a volunteer fire department.** You can tell a lot about a small town's sense of identity by how it solves its problems. For example, the town that looks to its larger neighbors for such basics as business promotion, fire protection, and other critical services has, in effect, become a bedroom community for its larger neighbor, and you will be in competition with the attorneys in that larger community. On the other hand, the small town that looks within—that actively promotes its businesses, and whose citizens are willing to look out for one another—is a community that is more likely to look for its attorneys locally before looking elsewhere.

**Look for a town that will be in need of a lawyer.** Look for a town with an aging population of lawyers rather than no lawyers at all. An aging population of lawyers means that there may be practices for sale, and buying into an existing practice can be a quick way to jump-start your rural career. For details, turn to Chapter 19 (*Should You Buy a Practice?*). Generally, any town where at least two-thirds of the lawyers are likely to retire in the next 10 years should be considered a town with an aging population of lawyers. Another suggestion: unless you are taking over an existing firm and have created some sort of "of counsel" relationship with the former owner, it will be far more difficult as the town's only lawyer to find mentors and advisors than it would be if the town has a population of lawyers nearing retirement. Young lawyers are usually too busy building their practices to be truly effective mentors.

Always keep in mind that choosing a small town usually comes down to a compromise; a balancing of needs and wants, of ideals and reality. While the numbers seem to indicate that your best chances are in the small towns of North and South Dakota, Arkansas, Kansas, Iowa, Idaho, Wisconsin, New Mexico, Indiana, and Kentucky (the states with the fewest lawyers per capita), it is possible to find your ideal rural spot in any state. See Chapter 10 (*My Own Rural Haven*).

## CHAPTER 8

# Life in a Small Town

*"Of all the pros and cons about a rural practice, the biggest pro is that I know everyone in town, and the biggest con is that I know everyone in town. It's tough when you're asked to represent a party in a case where you are neighbors with them both."*—Mindy Rush Chipman (class of 2007)

**S**mall towns are unique places. They're an entity unto itself, each a collection of rugged individualists who, because of some strange confluence of the stars, usually manage to live together in something approaching harmony on a particular patch of ground.

As you begin spending time in small towns, you find a single common denominator: at the core of small town life, these people…in this place…have figured out how to create a community that works for them, a community that somehow integrate even the most eccentric, whether it is the couple who keeps a puma as a house pet, or the mildly crazy sculptor who works in odd bits of plastic and trash (from neighbors' bins), or the guy who can repair anything and keeps the odd car (or cars) in his front yard, or the local restaurateur who dresses to match her establishment's decor (a style best classified as Early Brothel).

### Small Towns: A Study in Contradictions

People are the heart and soul of a small town. Things are not left to anonymous civil servants or elected bureaucrats; responsibility is in the hands of friends and neighbors. Small towns are places where you probably know the mayor, and meet him at his day job running the hardware store or the local feed mill. The same will be true with the members of the town council and the fire department. In fact, don't be surprised if the only full-time governmental employees are the city clerk, the sheriff, the postmaster, and (sometimes) the manager of the local liquor store.

☛ **Life in a small town adjusts its pace by the seasons and the weather**

Life's pace tends to speed up as the weather warms; summers are busy, filled with fairs, festivals, and family gatherings. Fall is full of preparation as shorter days and cooler temperatures remind us that winter is near. Small towns tend to hibernate, or at least slow down, in winter, waiting for the rebirth of activity that comes with spring. Spring is the best time to begin to find your place in a small town; there is something about a small town spring that makes people friendlier and welcoming. In summer, you will be seen as just another tourist; autumn is just too busy for much chit-chat; and no one is out and about during the winter (though winter is the time to buy a home because the prices are the most affordable).

☛ **Life in a small town is a study in contradictions**

What you see at first are the quiet roads, the green pastures, the quaint farms, the villages that could have served as models for Norman Rockwell's vision of America. What you don't see is that the spring thaw can turn those quaint country roads into quagmires capable of sucking the axles off an SUV; come summer, that quiet brook might breed mosquitoes the size of small aircraft that turn a summer evening into an exercise in chemical warfare.

☛ **Small towns are places for rugged individualists**

You will also find that, despite being one of the last bastions of true individualism around, small towns are dogmatically conformist, practically intolerant of any deviation from their strict notions of behavior and comportment. This dedication to conformity is what creates *community* in a small town. This singular focus provides the critical element for small town perpetuation, namely being a place where adults can live quiet, productive, satisfying lives, and raise children in a safe environment. The upside is that there are as many different variants of conformity as there are small towns.

☛ **Life in a small town is made up of small comforts**

It is about neighbors helping neighbors, saying hello to the stranger in the street, and of knowing that just about everyone will let you know when your children get into mischief (secrets are not something small towns are equipped to handle for long). It is also about realizing that slow traffic is likely to mean that there's a combine rumbling ahead, and that traffic at a complete standstill is a sure sign that two neighbors are in a deep discussion, their cars stopped, pointing in opposite directions, occupying both lanes of the road.

**Stranger in a Strange Land**

Compared to the typical suburban/urban experience, small towns should be considered a foreign land, each with its own unique identity, culture, and traditions. Don't be fooled by the fact that rural and suburban America share a common language and national culture. Small towns are firmly convinced that the way they do things is simple common sense, and is the right way to do things…even if it runs counter to an outsider's objective logic.

If your relocation is going to succeed, you must accept a different pace of life. Not necessarily a slower pace; instead, a pace that proceeds purposefully, deliberately, a conscious effort to be in synchrony with the town's rhythms. This is a pace that takes the time to play, to work, to talk, to be involved; it's about defining success by the quality of your relationships (private and public), regaining control over your life, and integration into a community rather than hours spent in the office.

☞ **As you settle into your small town, remember that business is not always about business.**

Take the time for small talk with those that stop by, and make room in your practice for small acts of kindness beyond the "free 30-minute initial consultation." This is not to say that you can't leverage this non-business business to your advantage. Small talk can always be a networking opportunity; just be subtle and discrete about it. And small acts of kindness can help you develop a reputation as being honorable (honor matters in small towns; these are places where your word is still your bond, and handshakes matter more than contracts). One thing to remember, these small acts, this kind of informal, impromptu, unadvertised and unprompted pro bono work, brings in business. Help someone's grandmother clear up a fraudulent credit card charge and you'll find her son paying you to handle a real estate transaction, or her granddaughter paying you to handle her divorce. So, change your initial consultation policy from "30 minutes and free", to "up to two hours for a charitable donation" and soon local charities are going to be referral sources. "*And will you succeed? Yes indeed, yes indeed! Ninety-eight and three-quarters percent guaranteed!*" (thank you, Dr. Seuss).

# CHAPTER 9

## Meet a Few Small Town Lawyers

*"A small town isn't for you if you prefer three-piece suits and depositions in plush conference rooms. But if you're a self-starter who wants to get your hands dirty—and make your own coffee—[a small town practice] is a great way to go."*—Bruce Dorner (class of 1977)

Novelist Thomas Wolfe once wrote that *you can't go home again*; that once you experience the grand and wondrous metropolis it's not possible to return to the simple, narrow confines of small towns. Well, that's one opinion. And yet an increasing number of big city lawyers are finding their way back to rural practices, back to family, back to places in the country, and back to a more relaxed way of doing things.

For some, like **Shane Penfield**[1] of Lemmon, South Dakota (pop. 1169), the journey from law school to rural practice was intentional. Shane did make a stop at a big law firm on the way, but he never doubted that someday he would return to his small town roots. In fact, Shane, a fourth generation Lemmon resident, credits his deep Midwest roots as a factor in his ready acceptance by the community, and his election to the office of County State's Attorney. For Shane, it was a way to balance his need to make a living while simultaneously building a practice.

From the small California coastal town of San Luis Obispo meet **Don Ernst**, an attorney who has earned a statewide reputation for his work representing plaintiffs in consumer rights cases. The former president of Consumer Attorneys of California was named the Central Coast Trial Lawyers Association's Lawyer of the Year twice (1998, 2002). Born and raised in San Luis Obispo, Mr. Ernst chose to return to his hometown after a brief stint as an associate in a large San Diego law firm. From his small town practice, he has taken on cases that have had significant statewide impact, including *Chastain v. Union Security Life Insurance* (a suit over a $4,000 credit card dispute that evolved into a three-year class action lawsuit affecting thousands of

Californians), and *Ratcliff v. The California Department of Corrections* (a gender discrimination suit resulting in a $3.34 million verdict for his clients).

In eastern Ohio, another small town lawyer is also doing big things.

**Lawrence Piergallini** (Tiltonsville, OH) has become the area's leading expert in shale oil leases representing more than 500 landowners, and helping them execute oil and gas leases covering 32,000 acres. Like most rural lawyers, Mr. Piergallini is an adaptive specialist. For the majority of his career, his practice focused on real estate and probate in an area where coal was king and coal leases were part and parcel of a real estate practice. With the oil shale boom roaring across Ohio's coal country, Mr Piergallini moved with the times and transitioned his practice to fit his clients' needs.

For others, the transition to small town practice comes about through interaction with rural clients while employed by Biglaw.

**Brooke Davis**[2] of Waxahachie, Texas (pop. 29,535) came to rural practice thanks to her interactions with small town clients while employed at a Dallas firm. Finding that rural clients were appreciative of her efforts on their behalf, were respectful of her time, and understanding that her family was a priority, Brooke decided to open a rural practice. Like most newcomers, she broke into small town society by being becoming involved in local activities, and by building a reputation for doing good work.

And for still others, it is the quiet, family-friendly lifestyle and affordability of small towns that lures them away from the siren song of Biglaw.

**Laura Mann**, drawn by the lower cost of living and the proximity to family, left a New York City commercial real estate firm for a solo practice in West Milford, New Jersey (pop. 26,410). Another advocate of the "getting-to-know-people" school of rural law firm marketing, Laura built her practice through community involvement.

There are as many paths to a rural practice as there are rural lawyers; some come to it straight from law school, some fall into it as a second career, and some because it is a better alternative to the big city/Biglaw way of life. The successful ones bring with them a sense of entrepreneurship, the ability to take on a bit of risk, and the willingness to become involved in their new community.

Case in point: **William D. Scruggs, Jr.** was a small town lawyer (Fort Payne, Alabama) who made a name for himself by representing clients in complex litigation, trying everything from murder and fraud to oil and gas. A year after his death in 2001, the Alabama State Bar created the William D. Scruggs Service to the Bar Award to honor his 19 years of service to the Bar as Bar Commissioner and State Bar President. In 2011 he was inducted in to the Alabama Lawyers' Hall of Fame.

## CHAPTER 10

# My Own Rural Haven

*"There is no magic checklist for finding the right small town even though the rankings suggested I would be happiest in a small city, I found the sleepy little town with one paved road to be far more livable. Go figure."*
—B. Cameron

Those small town ratings and ranking systems published in magazines and books don't tell you everything you need to know about a community's livability.

Since college, I have lived in four small towns and two small cities. And based on all those "how-to-find-your-ideal-rural-community" checklists and numerical ratings, I should have been happy in only one of the small cities. After all, it had growth potential, good health care, a large school system, two major employers, a thriving business district, outstanding public recreational facilities, and the city spent a small fortune on economic development. In fact, I lasted only about nine months there before heading to a small town whose schoolhouse closed in the 1960s, and whose "business district" consisted of three antique stores, a fishing boat store, one tavern, and a gas station. The only paved road was the one maintained by the county. Even though the small town ratings and ranking systems suggested I would be happiest in a small city, I found the sleepy little town with one paved road to be far more livable. Go figure.

In short, there is no magic checklist for finding the *right* small town for you, although the published rankings may help you narrow your selections and give you some means of weighing risk. After all, it is certainly better to open a law practice in a growing, vibrant town than one whose best days are past, and even better to start a practice in a locale where there is only one lawyer for every 2,000 people than if the ratio is 1:250. Of course, if the raw numbers were the only determinate for a happy, healthy small town law career, I'd be heading off to Martin, South Dakota.

At the moment, though, circumstances have me living just outside a small town, and practicing law from an office at the edge of a small city. For all the compromises (believe it or not, there are places in the country without a corner Starbucks), and the oddities of small town living, I find life here more manageable. Home is a place to relax, and time spent with my family no longer means juggling schedules to fit quality time around chores. And it is amazing how your blood pressure drops when it is no longer necessary to mow your lawn every time a blade of grass pokes above $2\,^3/_4$ inches as regulated by a neighborhood homeowners association. Sure, you have to put up with a few eccentrics (every small town has one or two), but remember they have to put up with you, too.

It's not ideal here. I still have to commute to my office, and it takes a more deliberate effort to market my practice to the rural community. But it is the best option that fortune has presented me to date. And yet, if I were deliberately looking for a small town to live and practice in, I would look for a town of about 1,500 that was located at the junction of a couple of state highways, and within a reasonable, 50-mile drive of at least three other small towns of similar size. While it would be nice if "my" town was also a county seat, I would willingly trade easy access to the courts for wide open spaces, and for being the only lawyer for an extended rural community of 3,000 to 4,500 people. It would be even better if I was one of just two lawyers so I would have someone with whom to talk shop at the local diner.

## Making the Transition

That old cliché that in a small town a stranger is anyone who hasn't lived there for three generations is not precisely true, but it *will* take some time for your small town to get comfortable with you, and for you to get established in your small town. So, to make that transition a bit easier, there are a few things you should keep in mind:

**Dealing with gossip.** In a small town, you are no longer an anonymous statistic, and as a newcomer you should expect that your presence will be a source of fodder for the rural grapevine: what you do and how you do it will get around and come back to you one way or another. Rural communities are adept at noticing and commenting on non-conformity. In our first foray into rural living, my wife and I quickly earned the appellation of "those hippy goat people" because (a) we were the only two registered Democrats in a town of 400 registered Republicans, and (b) we managed (what seemed to be) the largest goat herd in the area. *What we learned is that the key to minimizing gossip was to treat people with respect, fairness, and honesty.* Thus, when our neighbors discovered that we actually cared about the small town, and would take the town's side in political issues—AND were willing to learn farming from our more experienced neighbors—the appellation *hippy goat people* became more of a fond nickname than one of derision (though I was never sure that we were ever forgiven for being registered Democrats). Bottom line: small town people judge you by what they know about you. When gossip does not match their personal experience, the gossip goes away.

**Patronize local merchants.** Your law practice will be the new business on the block, and you're going to need ties to the local business community (if for no other reason than to build your referral network). *The fastest way to build those ties is to do business with local businesses.* The local lumberyard may not have the selection you might find at the national home-builder chains, but the local establishment does have ties to local contractors. The local hair salon may not offer that $10 haircut you used to get at your old discount clip joint, but it (and possibly the local bar) is rumor-central when it comes to the happenings around town. At the very least, patronize the local grocery, butcher, and farmer's market. They may not have the widest variety, but these businesses are gathering spots and they struggle to survive. Once they are gone, getting groceries will begin to look more like a cross-country expedition than a simple trip into town. Now, if you don't patronize local businesses because they don't offer a service you need or a product you want, that is understandable. But if you don't patronize them simply because you could save a few nickels elsewhere, you are fast on your way to earning a reputation as a cheap, uncaring SOB, not the best way to endear yourself to your new community.

**Donate to local causes and organizations.** *While financial donations are OK, the best thing you can give to a small town is your time.* Small town organizations and causes are always in need of help, and nothing will build community connections faster than working for a local cause. The key is to be involved, but not too involved; these organizations are not in need of your leadership; at least not until you've established yourself. Trying to jump into community leadership too soon is a good way to earn a reputation for being a condescending interloper. Instead, start at the bottom; volunteer to work the scrap metal pickup truck on Community Clean-Up Day, or direct traffic during the town's annual festival. Arrive early, leave late, and get a reputation for putting the cause (i.e., the community) first, and for going above and beyond what is necessary. After all, aren't these the qualities you want prospective clients to associate with your practice?

***Discretion should be your watchword.*** No matter how "quaint", "charming", or "precious" a small town may appear to your new eyes, never ever use those words to describe the town or anything relating to the town. The established residents will see it as (a) a mark of your naivety at best, or (b) downright insulting at worst. After all, how would you like the place you call home described in terms more often associated with those "charming", "precious" small dogs used as fashion statements? My recommendation is that for the first few years in a small town, you behave as you would at a long cocktail party: do your best to find common ground amongst a crowd of judgmental strangers, and avoid discussions of religion and politics until folks have gotten to know you. Remember, you have two ears and one mouth, and you can't go wrong by listening twice as much as talking. When you do talk, talk *with* people, not to them or at them. Don't try to sway them from firmly held beliefs (even if you know them to be misconceptions, and you have the weight of inconvertible evidence on your side). It will just earn you a reputation as a know-it-all.

Finally, *learn the art of self-deprecation. Small towns have a deep, almost instinctive dislike for a "show-off"*. So, if you roll into town with a car that costs more than the average house, and you wear suits to court that cost more the most folk's weekly salary, don't brag about it, and don't treat these items as anything special. Small town folk recognize quality and have a keen understanding that you can buy quality once or cheap many times, but that only social climbers advertise.

**Visit the author's Website at www.RURALLAWYER.com**

# CHAPTER 11

# In Their Own Words

### Q: What are some of the criteria by which you should select a small town?

*"Meet with local officials and see what the growth projections are for the area. Is there a 'one industry' situation where if that plant or facility closes the whole town goes dry? Does everyone sleep there and work elsewhere? Will you be in a position to work regular hours, or will you need to be open nights and weekends to serve the local population? How many banks are in town? [All] this often indicates that there is a lot of financial activity."*—BRUCE DORNER (CLASS OF 1977)

*"A lawyer should select the same small town to live and to practice. In addition to all the criteria that you would select a place for you and your family, also look at how the local government operates and the level of community involvement in the town. It is also helpful to select a small town that is near other small towns/rural communities. I am willing to drive up to 40 minutes, so I am able to handle cases in at least three other counties. I think having a central location is key. I am not talking about [being] in the middle of town, but [be] "close" to many different counties/districts."*
—MINDY RUSH CHIPMAN (CLASS OF 2007)

*"Make sure the community fits your practice area. For example our office is 45 minutes to an hour away from the two closest court houses. It would not make sense for us to have a primarily criminal/litigation firm where it take up to two hours to appear for a motion, status conference, etc."*
—JOHN THRASHER (CLASS OF 1993)

*"[Questions to answer]: what is the R (retail) factor of the community? Does it still have a high school, and will it have a high school in five years? How close is the court house, how long have the other lawyers in town been there,*

45

*and how old are they? Does the community try to attract business, or are they just hanging on? How many young people stay in the community?"*
—Pat Dillon (class of 2003)

*"An attorney should choose a small town to which he [or she] has ties already. If not, look for a community with a vibrant business community."*
—Shawn Sween (class of 2004)

### Q: Can you set up a rural practice on a shoestring?

*"You need a copier, a desk, malpractice insurance, a computer, and an Internet connection. It takes about 10K. Is that shoestring?"*—Pat Dillon (class of 2003)

*"Yes. No one expects me to look like a big firm so I am able to get away with doing most everything myself. I designed my own logo, website, business cards, letterhead, Christmas cards, etc. I know that DIY is not the best choice for marketing a law practice (just like we do not recommend clients represent themselves in court). However, I feel like my clients appreciate the fact that I am a) talented enough to even attempt these things myself, and b) frugal enough not to get trapped up in a ton of expenses."*—Mindy Rush Chipman (class of 2007)

### Q: What skills would help a lawyer adapt to small town life?

*"The small town attorney needs to be able to advocate for his client while recognizing the larger issues beyond the law, and how the client's legal solution will impact their position in the community. Sometimes a legal win is a larger loss to the client in the impact it has on the community."*
—John Thrasher (class of 1993)

*"You need to know how a business runs in order to operate a small office. If you don't understand basic buying and selling you're in trouble. And look for the practical solutions to the problems clients present. Often the fix is not legal, but just looking at other options. Being able to listen, sort out the facts from the emotion, and look for methods to get everyone in a more comfortable position is the key."*—Bruce Dorner (class of 1977)

### Q: What business and practice issues are important to consider?

*"Make sure you have a source of income sufficient to keep you from going into the hole, or that you have resources in the bank to carry you over the slower times."*—Bruce Dorner (class of 1977)

*"You need business management, accounting, and tax skills. Also you need to be good at creating systems and work flow."*—Fred Peet (class of 1993)

*"[In a small town], loud Hawaiian prints and pierced ears for men aren't going to get you a solid rural practice (outside of criminal defense)."*
—Pat Dillon (class of 2003

*"The biggest business / practice issue in my small town practice is having trouble trying to help too many people, feeling sorry for too many people, and eventually not billing enough for my work."*
—Mindy Rush Chipman (class of 2007)

## Q: Can a rural lawyer be a specialist?

*"Yes; I have a statewide practice in construction law which means that I do a lot of document review, materialmen lien filing, payment bond claims, and commercial collections so I am not dependent on local clients. I also represent several national companies with all their legal needs in Georgia."*
—Mark Cobb (class of 1991)

*"I know that I'm a general practitioner, and I have a lot of knowledge in a lot of areas. However, if things get deep, I'm not afraid to call one of my colleagues who works in that area of law for support or to refer the case. I suggest that, if possible, [you] pick one or two areas and become the so-called expert. But make sure there's enough business to keep you afloat…and be prepared to retool about every 5–10 years as new legal areas evolve."*
—Bruce Dorner (class of 1977)

*"A niche law firm is one way to make yourself stand out and make your work/life balance much more manageable. However, one aspect of being a small town lawyer that I still enjoy is being to help so many of your community members with so many different legal situations. I'm getting great exposure to many different areas of the law and, hopefully, making a difference in many peoples' lives."*—Mindy Rush Chipman (class of 2007)

*"I [know] a guy who does very little but Bankruptcies in my area, and makes a good living. Another guy does nothing but court-appointed criminal defense and seems satisfied. [As for me], I can't imagine saying I would only take real estate matters or only do estate planning. I can see [deciding] to not take litigation matters, personal injury, or workman's comp cases, but the basics of small*

*town practice are taxes, business, real estate, and probate. Hard to see functioning effectively in a town without addressing some of those areas."*
—Pat Dillon (class of 2003)

*"While a small town lawyer certainly could focus on one area of the law, I think he would have to reach outside the rural area to do so. I can imagine an attorney with a specialized focus setting up shop in a rural area because he likes the quality of life, but* [only because he] *solicits clients from throughout the state or nation. The fact is, there aren't as many people in rural areas, and it would be hard to maintain a niche practice while only serving a very small percentage of the local population's legal needs. Personally, I have found that rural people expect a rural lawyer to be able to handle most of their general legal needs. This means I need to be proficient in the basic areas that people need regularly—real estate transactions, wills and estates, and such small business transactions as formation issues, contracts, and debt collection. Then there are issues specific to rural areas, including agriculture and small community banking."*—Shawn Sween (class of 2004)

# SECTION III. A DAY IN THE LIFE

## CHAPTER 12

# The Rural Client

> *"Some clients want to run the show and tell you how to handle the case. [Other] clients tell you that a lawyer friend told them you should handle the case in a particular fashion. When I hear that I say, 'Let's get the friend (or lawyer) on the phone to discuss the situation.' Nine times out of ten, the friend or other lawyer is a myth. In the one out of ten times, I enjoy the conversation as I may learn something, or at least rule out that solution since the friend or attorney didn't have all the facts."*
> —Bruce Dorner (class of 1977)

Folks who live in small towns tend to be individualists, and generally the only thing they have in common is an (unspoken) belief in personal responsibility, and the ability of the citizenry to control their governance. These are honorable, stand-on-your-own-two-feet kind of people.

Sure, every small town is going to have a big helping of eccentrics, odd-balls, slackers, loafers, crazies, and idiots, but the vast majority of them are just good folks. They're the sort of do-a-deal-on-a-handshake, lend-a-neighbor-the-shirt-off-their-back, I'll-solve-my-own-problems kind of folks. And therein lies the problem; deals *are* done on handshakes, and people do assume the other party will be honorable and do the right thing. So don't be surprised when a client wants to open a probate two years after the decedent's death and three days before they want to close on the sale of the decedent's house, or they want to cancel a contract for a deed seven-and-a-half years after the last missed payment, or they need representation in a custody matter two weeks after the first hearing and 48 hours before the next, or they need to file a mechanics lien 115 days after the last day of work (note: in my neck of the woods, there is a 120-day window in which to file; your mileage may vary).

The fact is, dealing with the average rural client is enough to turn your hair prematurely grey. So, it behooves you to educate your client-base that the sooner they get a lawyer involved, the less costly the mess will be. When talking to groups like the chamber of commerce or union meeting, I often say, *"Letting me go over your deal before you shake hands will cost $100, and having me clean up a mess afterward will cost $10,000."* Repeat this often enough to enough people and you'll slowly change their behavior. My last mechanics lien matter actually came in with 60 days remaining in the window. The other thing is to make it easier for the client to be proactive than reactive. For example, I've found that sending out business-appropriate disclaimers (e.g., a mechanics lien disclaimer to a contractor) or, as a loss-leader, offering contract review at a fixed-price, go a long way toward encouraging potential clients to come in earlier rather than later. Also, by making sure that my clients know what they should be doing, and what information and documentation they should keep from the outset, makes my job simpler if everything goes south.

### Oh, the People You Meet

Rural clients are best described as radical conservatives, and the new rural lawyer is best advised to find out early on what their potential clients' views are on the institution of "attorney".

When I decided to open my practice, I had the great idea that I could leverage the Internet, have a virtual office, and meet clients in their own homes or place of business. My "hook" would be *no extra charge for house calls*. The beauty of the idea was that I could spend my days in comfortable jeans and baggy t-shirts, resorting to the three-piece lawyer uniform for house calls and court. I could work in comfort and save on my overhead. Then I started asking potential clients what *they* thought of their lawyer making house calls, of paying bills and scheduling appointments over the Internet, of having 24/7 access to information on their matter. Their responses were *unanimous*: these new ways of doing things would be nice if one was old, infirm, disabled, or house-bound...but they would never use them. But I really knew I was barking up the wrong tree when a 90-year-old neighbor told me that my ideas would be great if one were old, infirm, disabled, or housebound...but *he* wouldn't use them. After all, he only retired from farming at 85 because he broke his back in his youth, and the spinal fracture was finally "bothering" him. Did I mention that most folks in rural areas are independent, self-reliant, and tough?

So, what I discovered from my informal survey is that when my rural clients think "attorney", they have a mental picture of oak desks in quiet, mahogany-paneled offices; of three-piece suits, leather briefcases, and polished dress shoes; of fountain pens and yellow legal pads. While my rural clients won't say no to the occasional house call, they generally want to find their lawyer behind a desk in an office on Main Street because that is where one traditionally finds lawyers. Now, there is some logic behind this. Folks who live in small towns and rural areas tend to be fiercely private people and rural families are often multi-generational. It is not uncommon for grandparents, parents, and kids to be living on the same property if not under the same roof, and having a lawyer stop by to see grandma at home is going to set the kids wondering if she is changing her will when, instead, she just needed some help with a traffic ticket she got last week. So, the lawyer's downtown office symbolizes privacy and confidentiality. Also, going into someone's place of business ranks low on the list of small town gossip triggers, whereas doing something "non-traditional" is sure to get noticed by Mrs. Grundy.

The other thing that comes to mind when rural clients think "attorney" is "expensive". It is an image for which I must thank television, because after decades of TV programming, rural clients firmly believe that lawyers are high-priced commodities; furthermore, that only the very rich can afford lawyers willing to make house calls. So, my idea of making house calls was not considered a convenience; instead, it was a sign that I was going to be expensive, very expensive. My ideas on running a cost-effective practice simply did not meld with the expectations of my potential clients, and were politely rejected.

## What Rural Practice is All About

If you listen to tech-savvy pundits, the age of the transactional lawyer will soon come to an end as cloud-based, artificial intelligence software begins producing all the legal forms a person could ever want, at prices so low no lawyer could ever compete.

I have no doubt that software can produce a legal form correct in all particulars; that clever engineers can create an interface that asks all the necessary questions so that the form complies with statutory requirements. But this cheap, elegant, correct form will be *totally unsuited to a client's specific situation*. That is not what a law practice, especially a rural law practice, is all about. A rural law practice is not about the "product"; those forms, those missives of legalese that we lawyers produce on behalf of our clients.

Practicing rural law is not just about asking the necessary questions, it is about asking the right questions, and understanding not only what the client wishes to accomplish but also why before we move on to the how. Among family law lawyers, there are oft-told stories about the spouse who asks—and gets—the family home in a divorce settlement, and then turns around and sells it within the year simply because they could not afford the property on a single person's income. This is a classic example of understanding the what-a-client-wants part of the equation while ignoring the why. Understanding the why allows the lawyer to function as councilor not just as an advocate, and opens up the possibility of other options that may provide a better outcome and a better service to the client. Technology will always get the what, but it is unlikely to ever get the why, and therein lay its weakness.

A rural law practice (for that matter, a solo or small firm practice) is about service; service to clients, service to community. Technology, even the most sophisticated AI software, can't provide service; it simply cannot make that intuitive leap that uses both "what" and "why" to get to "how". And the lawyer who forgets that his or her true value lies in service not in product will not last long in rural practice. If you provide quality service and market your practice on the value you provide you need not be concerned about being replaced by CheapLegalForms.com.

**Visit the author's Website at
www.RURALLAWYER.com**

# CHAPTER 13

## Fees & Consultations

*"The key to having a successful law practice is to make sure that the amount of money coming in at the end of the month is greater than the amount of money going out, and you don't have to charge the same fee for every matter or to every client. Your fees just need to be reasonable."*

—B. Cameron

The tried-and-true method of determining fees is to charge an hourly rate, a practice that works if you don't mind the mindless tedium of tracking your time, and you accept that you will never track all of your time.

It took me three years to come to the realization that hourly rates were not working for me or for my clients, so I moved to a fixed-fee model. Clients like the certainty of knowing what a service (or portion of a service) will cost. If you are thinking about a fixed or alternate-fee model, the place to start is Ronald Baker's *Pricing on Purpose: Creating and Capturing Value*. But however much you charge for your services, you will not be able to charge big city rates in a rural setting. Even if you are the only lawyer in town, charging big city rates in a small town will have your potential clients rethinking that commute into the city.

Now, there are many books, Web sites, business coaches, and the like, who can provide learned discussions on the relative merits of various ways you should charge for your stock in trade. As near as I can figure, the key to having a successful law practice is to make sure that at the end of the month the amount of money coming in is greater than the amount of money going out, and the key thing to remember is that you don't have to charge the same fee for every matter or to every client. Your fees merely need to be *reasonable* (see your state's version of Model Rule 1.5 for the factors that determine reasonableness).

## Consultations

The standard "pizza"-style initial consultation (30 minutes & free) works about as well in small towns as using raw meat as shark repellant.

With most of your clients, it probably will take 30 minutes just to get through the "how-are-you's" and "what's new." So, what's a new small town lawyer to do? Well, you can always stick to tradition: give away 30 minutes and charge for the rest. But remember, the client is going to think that the consultation begins when they start talking about their problem, not when they first sit down with you. So, you could eliminate the small talk (which comes across as rude), you could be up-front and direct with what a client should expect (which comes across as pushy), you could charge for the consultation (it acts as a screening mechanism, which could be good, or it might make you look predatory, which would be bad), or you could just accept that your initial consultation is really going to take a more of your time and just take the hit.

Then again, you could try something a bit different. My solution was to adopt a technique I call "free-plus."[1]

The idea is that the first 30 minutes of a consultation are free, and for a donation to a local charity the client gets up to two hours of my time. I keep a bunch of envelopes pre-addressed to local charities and contain a pre-printed card stating that the enclosed check is a charitable donation. Clients choose an envelope, and they have the option of either writing a check directly to the charity or, if they wish to remain anonymous, they write the check to me and I write a check to the charity. It is up to the client to decide the amount of their donation. While I will suggest an amount if asked, I try to avoid suggesting one. This is simply a free-will donation. Sure, some folks scam the system, but most make generous donations within their means. Once the preliminaries are done, I sit down with the clients, and their matters proceed at the client's pace. This way, the client gets to decide how much of my time they want to use (I have yet to have a client use more than an hour), and, perhaps subconsciously, how they will use it. With very little effort, I get an opportunity to reinforce my referral network and an opportunity to build good community relations. As you set up shop, don't assume that just because something works in the "big city" it will work out here. Ask yourself, is this something where a little innovative thinking can result in a better experience or not? In a small town, almost every action has the potential for side-effects (aka gossip), and the challenge is to leverage them to your advantage.

## CHAPTER 14

# What Kinds of Cases?

*"A niche law firm is one way to make yourself stand out. [But] one aspect of working in a small town lawyer is being to help so many of your community members with so many different legal situations. I'm getting great exposure to many different areas of the law and, hopefully, making a difference in many peoples' lives."*—Mindy Rush Chipman (class of 2007)

The rural lawyer tends to be something of a generalist simply because he or she is often the only game in town.

The trick to being successful is to (a) develop a breadth of knowledge, and (b) know when to go to a mentor for support, or to refer the case to a colleague with the required expertise. The good news is that a small town's legal needs are fairly predictable; in most cases, these are going to be small, humble, one-off people problems, not large complex corporate problems. Even better, you don't have to take every matter that walks through the door. Don't want to do DUI defense? Don't.

To be profitable, though, a rural lawyer should expect to write wills, handle divorces and real estate closings, manage probates, defend misdemeanors, incorporate businesses, file liens, negotiate contracts, mediate conflicts, provide estate planning, resolve landlord-tenant issues, file bankruptcies, handle post-dissolution matters, and advocate effectively and litigate thoughtfully. The point is, you are going to be dealing with the "small letter" areas of the law; not Family law or Business law per se, but rather family law and business law. All those messy, nitty-gritty bits of law that families need (wills, divorces, buying and selling property, etc.), and those seemingly inconsequential matters that small businesses/business owners need (contracts and contract review, mediation, succession planning, etc.).

A word of caution: do your best to tailor your practice to your small town. If your community has one tavern for every 50 adults, it's a good bet that DUI defense is going to be a profit center, and perhaps you can forego elder law. Then again, if your small town happens to be a magnet for retiring boomers, start thinking estate planning, elder law, and medical assistance as your main revenue-generators rather than divorce and bankruptcy.

> *"While a small town lawyer certainly could focus on one area of the law, I think he would have to reach outside the rural area to do so. I can imagine an attorney with a specialized focus setting up shop in a rural area because he likes the quality of life, but [only because he] solicits clients from throughout the state or nation. The fact is, there aren't as many people in rural areas, and it would be hard to maintain a niche practice while only serving a very small percentage of the local population's legal needs. Personally, I have found that rural people expect a rural lawyer to be able to handle most of their general legal needs. This means I need to be proficient in the basic areas that people need regularly—real estate transactions, wills and estates, and such small business transactions as formation issues, contracts, and debt collection. Then there are issues specific to rural areas, including agriculture and small community banking."*—Shawn Sween (class of 2004)

## On Being a Specialist

Ask 10 different practicing rural lawyers if it is possible for a rural lawyer to specialize in a single area of law and you get 11 different answers. The consensus is that it is possible to concentrate on two or three practice areas, but the simple imperative of earning a living means that you will be taking unrelated matters occasionally. Think of it this way, being a small town lawyer is a niche in and of itself, and by its very nature attracts a limited client base; any further specialization may reduce that client base below the level that can sustain a practice.

So, in what way might a rural lawyer specialize?

Well, it depends on the small town you pick.

If you are going to limit your practice to a couple of practice areas, the odds of succeeding increase if there are other lawyers close by. The rationale here is that it is a lot harder to be recognized as an expert if the only person capable of recognizing that expertise is two counties over. Remember, though, most rural lawyers tend to be generalists, and are quite capable of handling the routine, so—as a specialist—your initial referrals are going to be the tough ones, the problematic, and the esoteric. Specialists are assumed to have a depth of knowledge and are capable of creating gold from dross.

As the other local lawyers become comfortable with you and confident in your abilities, they will start referring the more routine matters to you. It's going to be those lawyer referrals that will cement your reputation as the "go-to guy", the expert in a particular field. To the average rural client, lawyers are fungible; if they have a legal problem, they will talk with the local lawyer (usually the first local lawyer they run into) plain and simple. If you turn away too many of these "walk-in" clients because this is not the type of law you practice, you will soon have a reputation as being cold, uncaring, or unhelpful. So, at least in the beginning, take some of those mundane matters, and let the word of mouth from those lawyer referrals build your reputation as being the "one" for matters within your chosen specialty.

## A PEEK INTO MY CRYSTAL BALL

For the foreseeable future, there will be jobs for those lawyers who are willing to take a risk and head out to the sticks. Of course, my crystal ball gets a bit murky when it comes to knowing exactly what will be the "hot" areas of rural law as these trends tend to be fairly regional. Still, here is my prediction: the future rural lawyer can expect more client activity in **energy** (shale oil, gas, and wind leases), environment (water rights, land use, industrial impact), **Native American issues** (gaming, land rights, sovereignty), **agriculture** (genetically modified crops, feedlot and other regulations, wetlands), and **municipal law**. And then there is the serendipity of stumbling across The Next Great Thing simply by observing your rural community.

Basically, though, the big legal challenges will lie in places that have high potential for conflict, and in rural communities most hot button issues come down to the delicate balance between progress, preservation, and individualism, and how it is managed. The small town that fails to move forward and embrace new businesses is on the slow train to economic death, but if it fails to preserve those things that are essential to its community identity it risks becoming just another generic stop along a two-lane highway and there, at this intersection, lies opportunity.

The Forces of Progress will, of course, bring their own lawyers, lobbyists, and press agents, which leaves the rural lawyer to be the Voice of the Small Concerns, representing landowners, advising town councils, and being the advocate for small community organizations. This is job that calls for creativity as much as it does for legal acumen. The rural lawyer of the future should be versed not only in the traditional legal skills but in mediation and community conflict resolution because—more often than not—the necessary balance will not be found in the courtroom, but across the negotiation table.

## CHAPTER 15

# Get Paid Up Front (and 10 Other Lessons)

*"Don't underestimate your opponent. Rural lawyers are a collegial bunch outside the courtroom…but inside they are just as competitive as any metropolitan attorney, and they will do all they can to cut your carefully prepared case into ribbons."*—B. Cameron

There are 10 lessons that, if executed precisely and in the proper sequence, will guarantee that your small town law practice becomes a successful, profitable enterprise. Unfortunately, the only person who ever knew the secret also promised a recipe for turning lead into gold. In short, there is no secret sauce, no shortcut to success; you will have to be satisfied with these few modest suggestions to ease your way between failures:

☛ **Lesson #1: Get paid up front**

Discussing fees and collecting a retainer is the first of many difficult conversations you will have with clients. It is something that must be done, and it is necessary if your practice is to thrive. It is far easier to get paid up front than to try to collect when all is said and done. How much of the fee you ask up-front depends on your practice area, your client base, and your philosophy on retainers. Some attorneys feel that asking for any up-front payment casts a pall over the attorney-client experience; that it puts the focus on the cost of the service rather than on the *value* of the service. Another school of thought is that, if you aren't collecting fees you are essentially doing pro bono work…and that that is an expensive way to fail slowly. I've tried both methods of billing, and had clients stiff me under both (though not getting a final payment is a little easier to swallow if I got something up-front). For some practice areas—bankruptcy and criminal defense come to mind—full payment up-front is practically de rigueur and some, like real estate closings, lend themselves to payment at the end. For all those in-between situations, the right solution will be the one that best meets your and your client's needs. Just remember, if you develop a reputation for providing value most rural clients won't quibble about the cost.

### ☛ Lesson #2: Give it everything you've got

Until you are established as a fixture in the community, you and your business will be constantly evaluated, weighed, and measured. You will always be building your reputation, so give your law practice everything you've got and use every skill you have. This is more than just a reminder about working hard. Small towns make no distinction between the profession and the professional: what you do is part and parcel of who you are, so accept that you are going to be a lawyer 24/7/365 regardless of your office hours. After you are established as a fixture in the community, you will still be a lawyer 24/7…you and your practice will *still* be evaluated, weighed and measured… and you will *still* have to maintain your reputation. But at least now folks will have funny stories about you with which to tease you. This is a good sign; it means you've been accepted.

### ☛ Lesson #3: Stick it out

Prepare for the long haul. It will take time to build your reputation, your referral network, and your client base. And remember, half of all new businesses fail in the first five years of existence. So, watch your cash flow, consider alternate sources of income if necessary and, when things get tough, don't forget to call on friends, mentors, and your local equivalent of Lawyers Concerned for Lawyers. Sometime it only takes a single phone call to turn a month around.

### ☛ Lesson #4: Don't assume

Be observant, and learn about your small town and your potential clients. Is it a place with people that welcome innovation, or should tradition be your watchword? Never assume that your idea of innovation is the same as the others in your small town. Never assume that innovation will be welcome. On the other hand, don't assume that just because something has never been done that it can't be done.

☛ **Lesson #5: Invite people**

If you are going to build your business, you must meet people. You need people to be mentors, referral sources, and clients. In most small towns, once the Welcome Wagon has dropped by, any sort of outreach is up to you. So invite people to lunch, to a ball game, to an open house. Extend yourself; get out there and meet folks.

☛ **Lesson #6: Locate downtown**

If possible, set up shop downtown, preferably along the town's equivalent of Main Street. Downtown is where "local" businesses congregate. The big box stores, franchise chains, and other "foreigners" tend to sit on the fringe of towns, "in town" but not a part of the town. In a vibrant small town, downtown is where people meet, where festivals are held, and where things happen. People *drop by* downtown businesses, but merely shop at businesses on the fringe. If you want to work out of your home, it will take some prep work and you need to check local zoning codes before hanging out your shingle. Remember what I said earlier: rural folks value the formal trappings of a lawyer's office: *To rural clients, working from home is associated with those mail order businesses that advertise in the classifieds of such notable journals like "Grit" and the "Police Gazette"…but not legal professionals.* Still, if you do want to work out of your home, make sure to keep office and personal space separate. Ideally, have a separate entrance and a separate phone line; at a minimum, teach your family to answer the phone in a professional manner, and try to locate your office immediately off the front door. People will tolerate the occasional child-related emergency, but general interruptions should be kept to a minimum.

☛ **Lesson #7: Don't underestimate your opponent**

Generally, rural lawyers are a collegial bunch outside of the courtroom…but inside the courtroom they are just as competitive and cutthroat as any metropolitan attorney. And just as interested in getting a "win" for their client as you are for yours, and they will do all they can to cut your carefully prepared case into ribbons. When the case is over, the adversarial relationship is also over. They may be your competition, but they should also be your friends. They are your best defense against feeling isolated and your best means of introduction to the people you should know. When you first arrive in town, they will be your source for those smaller cases that can get you started, and later they may refer their conflicts and overload to you.

## ☛ Lesson #8: Invest in your practice

First, never spend before you earn. Second, during your profitable months set something aside for those slow periods. Third, and very important, invest in the business "experience" of your law practice. The business experience is the reality your clients will perceive when doing business with you. It is those visceral, emotional, sensory cues that overpower your client from the moment they walk into your office to the moment they leave. It's this business experience that contributes to your brand, and forms the foundation of that oh-so-valuable thing called word-of-mouth marketing. If you really want to investigate the concept of the engineered business experience, read Lewis Carbone's *Clued In: How to Keep Customers Coming Back Again and Again*. Last but not least, invest in yourself by creating a comfortable space separate from where you meet clients. After all, you will be in the office for many long hours. You need a place that meets your needs; ergonomic office furniture, shag carpets or Persian rugs, some art work on the walls, orchids in the window sills—whatever suits your fancy.

## ☛ Lesson #9: Deal with gossip

In a business sense, gossip is one of your better marketing tools; it's free, it's direct, and it's fast. The trick is to make sure that it is accurate. So, if you are going to do something gossip-worthy, be open about it. Remodeling your office? Let the local newspaper know about your plans, leave the door open, and take the time to talk to those who drop by. Not just about what you do, but about the history of the building (if it's an old one), the history of the town, their family, etc. Take the time to make connections. Receive an important award? Have an open house; not to talk up the fact that you won an award, but to have a community event to mark a milestone moment.

## ☛ Lesson #10. Have regular hours

Folks will want to know what hours you keep. Your hours shouldn't necessarily be 9-to-5 Monday through Friday. In fact, you may be better off with hours that are outside traditional banking hours. Don't forget that from a client's point of view, your 9-to-5 schedule means their loss of a half-day's pay. Consider evening or weekend hours. It might be inconvenient for you, but it may make your clients' lives easier.

☛ **Lesson #11: Don't wait for clients to fire you**

Ethical obligations permitting, the time to fire a client is when you get that sinking feeling that the lawyer-client relationship is going south. Frankly, there are just some client-lawyer relationships that don't work, and a poor working relationship yields poor word-of-mouth. Better to rip the bandage off quickly than let things fester. Sure, you will have a dissatisfied ex-client. But by concentrating on your good clients, you'll have many more positive voices out there working for you. The corollary is to know when to say "no" to clients. There are many helpful hints online, and there are useful CLE's on how to avoid the client from hell. But saying "no" to a client is about more than just making your life easier; saying no, and then referring a client to a more experienced attorney or to one whose niche is a better fit to the client's needs, can be the best legal advice you can give.

---

**Visit the author's Website at
www.RURALLAWYER.com**

---

# CHAPTER 16

# The Rural Jurist & Small Town Courts

*"Rural judges tend to give the new lawyer a break. But make no mistake; this is a one-time, not-to-be-repeated gift, and you are expected to learn from it and learn quickly. And don't expect the judge to save you from flushing your case down the drain."*—B. CAMERON

Hollywood's mythic rural judge—portly, elderly, often bumbling—is a wholly inaccurate depiction of the rural judiciary.

In my experience, rural judges are as able and educated as their metropolitan counterparts, but often are different in two notable ways: rural judges are more likely to engage in small talk from the bench, and they are more likely to give the newly fledged lawyer a break...at least for awhile. It's a luxury that may disappear in these times of decreased funding for the courts and crowded court dockets.

But don't think that a rural court is filled with extraneous chit-chat.

The rural court is nothing but business, in all of its formal, equitable glory, and woe unto those attorneys who forget that. On occasion, the rural jurist may—between *"next case"* and *"call case number"*—may find the time to inquire about you, your family, your practice, etc., especially if it has been some time since you last appeared in court. Now, this is not intended as cocktail hour small talk; it's just a brief check-in between colleagues who have not seen one another in a while (and, by the way, *the Court* asks the questions; you answer them. It's not a two-way conversation).

Rural judges do tend to give new lawyers a break, whether it is providing a bit of time to collect one's thoughts, to correct a small error in a proposed order, or hearing the objection you should have made rather than the one you actually did make. But make no mistake; this is a one-time, not-to-be-repeated gift, and you are expected to learn from it and learn quickly. And don't expect the judge to save you from flushing your case down the drain.

There is a story (most likely apocryphal) about a young lawyer's first time in a rural court. The lawyer was so nervous that he couldn't begin his opening statement without stuttering. So, the judge recessed the court, and called the young lawyer to the bench. In a reassuring voice, the judge told the young lawyer that one's first appearance in a courtroom can be nerve-racking, but now that his first court appearance is over, he should take the next 15 minutes to collect his thoughts…because when the recess is over it will be his *second* court appearance!

## Courthouse Staff

Rural courthouses, like their metropolitan cousins, are ruled by their judges, but they are run by the clerks, registrars, and recorders, a competent and efficient group of people who are one of a small town lawyer's greatest resources. They have a vast trove of knowledge about the workings of the courthouse, and will be more than happy to tell you about preferred paper sizes, paper colors, font sizes and font types; whether you can mail, email or fax filings; what court costs and fees are, and all the sundry other bits of courthouse knowledge.

If approached politely, they occasionally will confirm which documents should be filed together, and in what order they should appear. But they will not provide legal advice (at times the distinction between the two situations eludes me, but they know where the line is and they don't cross it). My general approach is to prepare all the documents I think are needed, and then say to the clerk: "*I am new to the court and am going to file a _____, and I want to make your job easier…*" or, "*I have prepared the following documents: _____, and want to know what order you want them in and whether you need an original of _____ or will a copy do?*" Usually the clerk will give you the order in which they want the documents, and they may mention that copies are fine, or that they don't use Document A anymore, or that the judge prefers documents B & C to be combined, or they have their own special version of Schedule D, and would you use that, etc. Generally, a request for help works *once*…and only once… per section. That is, you can do the newbie thing once with the probate clerk, once with the scheduling clerk, etc. So pay attention, take notes and follow their advice. Rural courthouses are small and word gets around quickly. If you are going to ask for advice but then not take it, you'll find (usually the second time around) that no one will give you advice again. Also, remember your manners; *please* and *thank you* go a long way. Oh, and don't presume to use first names too quickly. Small towns tend to be old-fashioned in this regard, and, until a courthouse staff member gives you permission to use their first name, address them as Mr., Mrs., or Ms., followed by their surname. It also doesn't hurt to follow up with hand-written thank you notes or a short note of praise to an individual's supervisor.

This advice works better in some areas than others. On the one hand, the more transactional the matters handled by the department, the more willing the staff is to pass out small bits of advice. On the other hand, it never works if you're filing a matter for litigation. The clerks are going to assume that you either know what you are doing, or you have an experienced attorney as second-chair. In small town courthouses, litigation is serious business and everyone is expected to be up to speed on things from the word go.

# CHAPTER 17

# Marketing & Growing Your Rural Practice

*"As a rural lawyer you will be asked to do everything from DUI's to divorce, but it is hard for any solo/small firm to be the best at everything, and far more difficult to convince others of that fact. So, do one thing well for one well-defined demographic. Because without focus your marketing and your practice will lack direction."*—B. Cameron

**M**arketing the rural law firm is simple; you go out and talk with people. Every contact you have with the world outside the confines of your house and your office is marketing. Your business name, your business cards, your Web site, your phone number, the color and font used in your stationery, your office location, the quality of coffee you serve to the clients waiting in your lobby, the tone you use when answering the phone, your voicemail greeting, the time it takes you to return calls, your staff, your current clients, your former clients, the vendors you use, and the million and one other clues that form the entire experience that is doing business with you is all part and parcel of your marketing.

Your only goal should be to get to know people. Ideally, of course, you want to get to know people who have a problem you can help with. *But, in a small town, the person with whom you're talking may not have the problem, but may know someone who does.* That's why you have to get out there and be visible; have lunch with the local clergy, do a presentation on estate planning at the local senior center, attend the monthly chamber of commerce breakfast, meet a neighbor for coffee. To a rural lawyer, it's all marketing.

It may sound easy; it isn't. In fact, marketing in a small town might just be one of the hardest things to do successfully. It takes time and careful thought.

You have to be reaching out to your clients, your potential clients, your referral sources, and your potential referral sources, on a *regular* basis. Initially (i.e., for the first few years), marketing will be a daily task; as you become established, you can ease off a bit…to every other day. And once you become a town fixture (say, after a couple of decades of practice), your marketing efforts can trail off to about once a week. But at all times, you cannot stop thinking about who your ideal client is, and how you can reach those people who might come in contact with that ideal client.

## Marketing: It's *Not* About You

Marketing your services in a small town is *not* about you or your firm. It is about your opportunity to show current and prospective clients that you can help them achieve their goals.

Marketing is a cyclic process; there is a beginning and middle but there is no end. You may change tactics, you may modify strategies, you may develop new habits, but lawyer marketing is a continuous process that takes energy, time…and imagination.

The thing to remember is that once you start talking to people in terms that relate to your legal practice (if you do estate planning and start talking about the generation-skipping tax consequences of an unfunded revocable trust, or if you are a litigator and start describing the process of summons and complaint), client boredom sets in and your marketing effort will grind to a halt. If you are going to market your practice in a small town, skip the legalese, ignore your finely crafted processes, and have a conversation. Don't frame the conversation in terms of your job title or your experience; put yourself in the clients shoes, and frame the conversation in terms of the problems you solve and the solutions you provide in a way that is relevant to the audience with whom you're speaking (and if this means spending 30 minutes listening to how the crops are doing, your client will think you're a great lawyer).

Remember, marketing in a small town is about conversations. Real conversations.

***Marketing and rural networking.*** Networking for the rural lawyer is a fairly simple process; you get out and meet people, and you get involved in your community.

> "It all depends upon local custom and character. An online presence is essential. Having your name known in the community is important. And whether you get involved through religious organizations, charitable groups or community service, positive name recognition is critical. Offer to write short articles for the local free paper. See if the local cable TV station would like a few segments about new legal issues."—BRUCE DORNER (CLASS OF 1977)

But it's up to you to go out and meet folks, because after the visit from the local Welcome Wagon, most small town folks will assume that if you aren't going to meet them, you want to be left alone. And they will respect your privacy, and let you get on with your life. Starting points for networking are abundant, and they can range from inviting a neighbor in for coffee to attending Chamber of Commerce lunches, or joining the local Rotary club. Networking can be a passive, off-hour activity like writing for the local newspaper (small town papers are usually ravenous for free content; just be sure to write it plain English). Or, you can be quite active, like volunteering with the local fire department. Remember, though, networking isn't a one-off sort of thing; the newspaper will expect regular copy over a long-term, the fire department is going to want you to make all the meetings, and your neighbors are going to expect the odd chat every now and then.

☛ **Your goal is to create positive name recognition, and the time to start is the day you arrive in town.**

Make use of the fact that you are the new, exciting thing in town; leverage that curiosity, and be proactive in establishing how the town defines you. If you wait too long, the town will start defining you themselves, and it would be hard to overcome poor first impressions. In all your marketing and networking, what you are going for is not just the "when-you-think-of-Bob Smith-you-think-attorney" kind of name recognition. The goal is "when-you-think-of-Bob-Smith-think-reliable-competent-man-of-his-word-always-willing-to-give-you-the-time-of-day-attorney". That's the kind of name recognition you can take to the bank!

***Marketing your passion & personal service.*** People in a small town are just like people everywhere. They want to succeed; succeed at earning money, building a business, raising children, running their farms.

Your job is to show them that you can help them achieve those goals, and to make sure that every person with whom you come in contact leaves happy. How? By remembering small courtesies; sending thank-you notes to referral sources, sending reminder cards to clients about upcoming appointments, sending a short, "feel-free-to-call-on-me-if-I-can-serve-you-in-the-future" note even to those who didn't hire you. Marketing is about expressing the passion, personal service, and solutions that you bring to your practice. It is a continuous process that demonstrates your value to your target market by communicating how people profit from your services.

Lawyers often assume *their* concept of value, and their client's concept of value, are alike. Lawyers also tend to assume that value is a simple equation: good work at a fair price. But research indicates that *95 percent of what influences consumer choice occurs in the subconscious, and that it is the sensory and emotional elements of the entire consumer experience that influence customer preference, repeat business, and referrals.*[1]

The "good work/fair price proposition" focuses on the functional and the expected; after all, one expects their lawyer to do good work, just as one expects a car to start, and a refrigerator to keep things cold. The functional is easy to evaluate, market, and to sell; it is what we would like to think the consumer is buying. But the functional only addresses the rational, thinking brain, which means that it only addresses 5% of the decision-making process. The consumer's experience also includes personal factors (tone of voice, enthusiasm, body language, manners, etc.), and environmental factors (the sights, sounds, tastes, smells, textures, etc.) of the interaction. And these tend to be assessed and valued by the subconscious brain. It is this emotional bonding to the total experience—the functional, sensory, and emotional—that creates consumer value. Consider: if I'm buying a car, I might not mention that the reason I don't buy from dealer A is because the salesman's "I'll-be-with-you-in-a-minute" turned into a 20-minute wait, or—if I do buy the car—it's because I am fiercely loyal to their mechanic who always returns my car washed and vacuumed.

It's easy to understand how getting the *functional* wrong can kill a deal, but you can't overlook the touchy-feely elements.

***Marketing: a few basic truths.*** Marketing is part science, part art, and all business. Of course, the purpose is to earn profits AND to turn clients into raving fans. If what you are doing is not earning you profits, not bringing client in the door, not building you a network of fans (referral sources), then it's just not good marketing, and you should probably stop doing it. Marketing is about developing a basic set of habits and assets, and working from a continuously improving knowledge base. There are a few simple keys to good marketing:

- **Always follow up.** 70 percent of lost business is lost because of a lack of follow-up.[2] So, follow-up when a client contacts you. Send out appointment reminder cards, send out a thank-you letter after a prospect comes in for an initial consultation, and send out a summary letter after a client meeting. These notes needn't be elaborate, but you do have to make the effort; a First Class stamp is a small price to pay to get more clients.

- **Maintain your focus.** As a rural lawyer you will be asked to do everything from DUI's to divorce, but it is hard for any solo/small firm to be the best at everything, and far more difficult to convince others of that fact. So, do one thing well for one well-defined demographic. *Without focus your marketing and your practice will lack direction.* You'll lose track of what you are marketing, and how you market and to whom, and you'll wind up spreading yourself so thin that you won't get much of anything done.

- **Look for synergy.** Are there other businesses in your neck of the woods that deal with the same clients you do? Do these businesses have the same standards? If so, there might be an opportunity for you to cooperate with them in some joint marketing. After all, just because you are a solo doesn't mean you have to do everything by yourself. For example, say you do estate planning: why not team with a financial planner and an insurance agent and put on a community education class. You'll get to build a relationship with two local businesses, and all three of you get more exposure to more clients.

***Marketing begins with a plan.*** Your marketing efforts need to occur on two levels: a primary level (think retail) that reaches out to your ideal client directly, and at a secondary level (think wholesale), reaching out to your ideal client's *influencers* (those who influence your target client to buy a product or service). Primary marketing is about short-term strategies that are intended to bring your ideal client in the door now; secondary marketing are about long-term strategies intended to build relationships with influencers in a position to refer new clients…perhaps not today or tomorrow, but maybe in six months or a year.

Whether you're marketing to primary or secondary targets, you must develop a plan. The ideal plan should be consistent with your personal values and comfort levels; never force yourself to do something that your gut says is wrong (your passion will never show through if all you can think about is how nervous you are). You need to know why you are marketing (do you want more clients, more money, less work, etc.), to whom you are marketing, how you are going to attract these people, and what assets you can bring to this activity.

### Learning More About Your "A"-Level Client

What do you know about your "A"-level client?

You need to think beyond demographics (age, gender, income, education, type of employment, etc.). You need to also consider what they want (i.e., their emotional desire for security, resolution, control, guidance, relief, etc.). Get specific. It will help distinguish your practice from the competition. After all, yours may be the only practice in town, but there are other towns within driving distance, and you need to demonstrate how your solutions are the best match to the client's problems.

Knowing what motivates your ideal client, and who influences them, will help you to put the right marketing materials in the right place at the right time. Of course, consistency is the key. Everything you send out to your "A"-level market should communicate the same overall message: (1) the type of clients with whom you work, (2) the problems you solve, the solutions you provide, and the value you offer, and (3) what distinguishes you from the herd. There is no one-size-fits-all way to do all this; the actual message must be tailored to your immediate audience. *Sometimes the simple act of listening will be the most effective form of marketing.* That is, you let your ideal client educate you about their business, their clients, their problems, and the level of service they need/want rather than you giving them the ol' elevator speech. Part of knowing what to say is to know when not to say it.

**Some tools and skills.** When it comes to marketing, nothing should ever have a single purpose.

When you buy pens for the office, don't just buy generic pens; get pens branded with your name and phone number (every client should leave with one, and every time you sign a charge slip, leave your pen behind). Business cards? They shouldn't just contain your contact information; they should also provide links to Google Maps or your Web site. Your business cards should start conversations. Blogs? If you write a blog, why limit your posts to your blog; recycle them into newsletter articles or newspaper columns (even a self-published book). Leverage is your friend; it lets you get more mileage from each marketing asset. And don't forget to track everything. Know where each and every client inquiry comes from (is it from a referral source, your Web site, a flyer?). If it came from a referral source (an influencer), know who the source was. Know if the inquiry turned into an initial consultation, and if that initial consultation turned into a client. Know if your clients are satisfied. Ask them what you are doing right and what could be improved.

Start developing your marketing habits from the first day you set foot in a small town…and begin with the "thank you" habit. Send "thank you" cards to the folks who do nice things for you (like referring a potential client to you). In small towns, people appreciate good manners. The other habits you should develop are the "getting out" and "asking" habits. Get out and meet people. Try to meet five new people a week and have three significant contacts a week with people you already know. What's a "significant" contact? It's something more than a quick, "*Hi, how are you?*" as you pass in the street. A significant contact is when you take the time to have a chat about the weather, their kids, their business, their hobbies, etc. Oh, and don't forget to ask for a referral at the end of the conversation. If you don't ask, how will anyone know that you are looking? Your business thrives on referrals from people like them.

**Choosing the Right Medium**

It's not enough to just identify your "A"-level target, you need appropriate media to reach them. And the first marketing medium for consideration is a Web site.

Almost 80 percent of the US now uses the Internet, and while most small town clients usually go online for crop reports and livestock futures, they are more likely to turn to Google than the phone book when looking for products and services. And since the average reader spends a mere 8 to 12 seconds looking at a Web site, your site has to make it fast and easy for the reader to determine that you have the solution to their problem, how you can be contacted, and where to go for more information.

**Newsletters**. Newsletters remain a great tool for keeping your name top-of-mind. The key to a successful newsletter is focus and relevance. Your newsletter must be tailored to the reader's needs (a client newsletter will be different than one sent to your referral network), and each issue must offer clear, concise, interesting articles with a conversational tone. Remember, you are not writing for a law review. The other thing to remember is to not confuse quality with quantity. Unless you are practicing in a highly dynamic area of the law, a quality newsletter sent quarterly will be far more effective than one assembled hastily on a weekly basis.

**E-mail**. Your e-mail is not merely a medium for quick communication. It should also be a marketing tool. Treat it as your electronic letterhead and, at a minimum, it should carry links to your Web site, and v-card.

**Brochures, one-sheets, pamphlets.** These are all good vehicles to get information into general circulation. The idea is to develop a simple, easy-to-read, single-page digest of a given topic (*The Top 10 Questions about Your Will*, or, *The Four Things You Should Know about Real Estate Sales*). Brochures, one-sheets, and pamphlets are not in-depth exercises; they're best when they take the 30,000-foot view. The goal is to develop a library of pamphlets that cover the scope of your practice. They should carry your contact information, and adopt the same typography as the rest of your marketing materials.

But be subtle with your branding; you want the reader to pass your work to friends, family, and clients, and it is easier if the material does not scream, "this-is-lawyer-advertising".

**Questionnaires**. An often-overlooked marketing opportunity is your intake questionnaire. Think about the message you are sending when you send out that intake questionnaire. You are going to be asking the prospect to spend hundreds if not thousands of dollars for your services, and all you send is a simple cover letter that says, in effect, "Thanks for setting up an appointment, please fill out this form". Most health clubs send out more than that, and they're only asking for $20/month. What you want to do is cultivate the impression that by hiring your firm, the prospect is about to become a member of a very exclusive club, so why not send out a "welcome kit" rather than just a form. Your kit could include: a thank you letter, your intake form (branded, organized in a logic flow with some explanation as to why you need the information and how accurate the prospect needs to be), a few pamphlets relating to the client's matter, a book or a few articles or some other educational material (all marked with your contact information), a pen (branded, of course), and a few business cards. All of this should be tucked inside a branded folder. The idea is to provide the client with useful information (information that they can show around to their friends & family), and that they can use to educate themselves, and that you can refer to when speaking with them (*"This is a quick explanation of...there is a more in-depth explanation in the article in your Starter Kit"*).

**Business cards.** Another overlooked marketing tool is the simple business card. Thanks to the emergence of QR Codes (Quick Response codes are just two-dimensional bar codes), and the increasing use of smartphones (yes, even farmers and ranchers have joined the iPhone/Android generation), business cards can now do more than simply providing contact information. By incorporating QR Codes and using both sides of the card, business cards can be conversation-starters that provide links to your on-line marketing materials and other useful digital content (maps, Web sites, downloadable brochures, articles, etc).

**Social media.** Used correctly, social media can be a positive asset to your marketing efforts. It can increase your Web site's search engine position, it can increase top-of-mind awareness, and it can bring clients to your door. On the other hand, social media can be a huge time-sink that generates absolutely nothing. There are a couple of tricks to using social media profitably. You have to use the same social media outlets as your ideal client (and their referral sources). You don't have to use all the same outlets, but your social circles do have to overlap your clients. The second key to social media is consistency. Whatever you do, you have to do it consistently and regularly. If you blog, you should post monthly at least; if you tweet, do so hourly; if you're on Facebook, be there daily.

**Video**. Video can add a dynamic element to your Web site, and increase your search engine ranking at the same time. Think of video marketing as a form of one-sheet; a concise, high-level, 30-to-60-second topic summary. Producing your own Web videos doesn't require a lot of expensive technology. A digital camcorder, an external mic, and a quiet well-lit room is all you need. For editing, try MovieMaker (free with Windows) or iMovie (free with Mac OS). Use video to speak to your target market without lecturing. A good video should be somewhat informal, educational, and provide a little insight into your philosophy of practice. Have a script and do a little rehearsal; sounding "informal" takes a little practical. Your first video should cover something you are passionate about, something with which you are intimately familiar, and are extremely knowledgeable. How about a "welcome to my law practice" video? Once you start producing videos, don't forget to also post them to YouTube, it is the third most searched site on the Internet; right behind Google and Facebook.

**Giveaways**. Small, inexpensive, useful branded items like refrigerator magnets, mugs, shopping bags, and flash drives can keep your name and contact information in front of a prospect a lot longer than a business card. Giveaway pens branded with your firm name, logo, telephone number, and a short tagline, are especially useful marketing items. For example, a client comes in for a real estate closing, be sure to include your pen with the closing documents; you go out to lunch, leave a pen with your tip; buy gas, drop a pen in the can after signing the charge slip. The thing about pens is that they travel from person to person, and come with a kind of back-handed referral (I got this lawyer's pen from Bob, I know/like/trust Bob, Bob must think this lawyer is OK). Other small items (branded BandAids, letter openers) should be considered throw-away promotional items, a reward for attending a retail marketing event (a community ed class, a county fair booth, etc). High end swag (coffee mugs and flash drives) lend themselves well to an "if-you-sign-up-for-our-free-newsletter-today-we'll-give-you-a-free…" This way, you get contact information and permission to communicate with this person regularly; they get a coffee mug or flash drive. One word about flash drives: never give them away empty; stuff them with other marketing items (your v-card, one-sheets, pamphlets, etc.).

## Lawyer Advertising

Advertising is easier but more expensive than marketing, it has a far lower ROI (return on investment), and, more often than not, you can't count on advertising to bring in clients.

In my opinion, advertising is a matter of investing large amounts of money over long periods of time to remind the people who are already aware of you that you still exist. The hope is that this repetitive outreach will keep you "top-of-mind", so that when the need arises, your name is the first that comes to mind. The problem is, advertising is generally driven from the inside out; it is about telling people the things you want them to hear, and does little to demonstrate how your services will achieve a prospective client's goals. Furthermore, advertising is linear; a campaign has a beginning, middle, and an end, with little opportunity for follow-up (and, trust me, in rural communities, the lack of follow-up can lose you business).

The effectiveness of most forms of advertising (print ads, radio, TV) is hard to track and measure and serves more to reinforce your marketing efforts than as business-building tools. Ads can work, but they have to be targeted to a very specific market, and they have to link your name to the value you provide to a client. Yes, ads can build name recognition, but clients will probably not be able to remember that they learned about you from one of your ads. So, be prepared to spend several thousand dollars on an ad campaign, and *don't be surprised if there is only a minimal increase in the number of new clients coming to your door.*

For the small town lawyer, though, some advertising will be expected of you.

It might take the form of a sponsorship of a local youth sports team or Future Farmers of America club or 4H event, or the town's annual fair, or the volunteer fire department's dinner-dance. While local sponsorships are unlikely to result in a huge uptick in business, they are things that help to build goodwill in the community. You don't have to buy into every community-related sponsorship which comes along. But choose one or two, and then be consistent in your support. If you want to earn extra goodwill, get involved with the group. And if you REALLY want to maximize your return, be known for your modesty; don't act as if you deserve special treatment just because you're an event sponsor. Incidentally, the sponsor who also volunteers to spend the day of the event hauling trash or taking tickets gets far more positive buzz than the one who merely shows up for the t-shirt and the "thank you".

Of course, having a Web site or a blog is a given these days. Most of my clients view the Internet as a fast way to track farm commodity prices, and not as the default for information gathering or social contact. This may change as rural kids become as Web-savvy as their urban and suburban counterparts, and as broadband data and fiber optic connections reach further into the hinterlands.

## A Few Advertising *Don'ts*

Based on personal experience then, here are a few advertising *Don'ts* of which rural lawyers need to be aware:

- **Don't advertise in phone directories.** I have never found a phone directory ad to deliver a good return on investment. Even directories targeted at small towns will have a couple of pages of attorney ads at least. In my opinion, you get a better return on your advertising dollar if you put your print ad in the local newspaper, community magazine, co-op newsletter, or a value-pack mailer. But if you feel that the phone book ads are for you—and you don't have the budget for that full-page back cover—there are a few things that can make your ad more effective. First, don't make your ad look like all the other lawyer ads regardless what the salesman says. Remember, you're trying to disrupt the client's search, and to make them focus on you, so create an ad that stands out. In fact, data shows that *the best way* to do that is with text, lots of text; there is a direct correlation between the number of words in an ad and number of calls (double the words, double the calls). So, make your ad look like an editorial, an *advertorial* if you will, and use it to educate clients on the solutions you offer. Second, data also shows that while lawyers are happiest with big ads that include their photo, most clients skip those big fancy display ads and spend most of their time looking at the inline column ads that provides specific information (hours, location, etc.). *Bottom line:* look at your ad through a client's eyes: does it provide the information a client wants, does it allow the client to easily identify the solutions you provide, does it tell them how to reach you, and what next steps they should take?

- **Don't advertise in small organization-specific directories** (church directories, union directories, etc.) unless you belong to the organization or plan to interact with the organization's members on a regular basis. This means attending the odd church picnic, giving a talk or two to the union members, being there for the games the little league team you've sponsored plays. Then again, if you are taking the time to get involved with the community, this really isn't advertising at all; it's just another marketing opportunity.

- **Don't get listings on any online directory** unless it is (a) free and (b) you are able to cancel or delete the listing at your discretion. Your clients are unlikely to use any of these services so why pay for them. The only good reason to use these listing services is to drive search engines to your Web site. If you are going to incorporate them into your advertising plan, then it only makes sense to retain control over the content (including the ability to delete it).

The very best sort of marketing is to never stop pursuing excellence. While rural clients are always appreciative of the old "under-promise-and-over-deliver", pursuing excellence is more than just exceeding client expectations. It is also about exceeding your expectations for yourself. It is about being better tomorrow than you were today. Excellence builds reputation, reputation builds word-of-mouth, and word-of-mouth brings clients.

CHAPTER 18

# In Their Own Words

**Q: How important is community involvement in building and maintaining a small town practice?**

*"We are very active in the community. I think it is expected of us and gives us a chance to interact with a large segment of the community in a positive manner. Not only does it improve the community, but I believe it is the most effective form of [law firm] marketing in a small community."*
—John Thrasher (class of 1993)

**Q: What were you least prepared for in the beginning?**

*"I was least prepared to deal with accounts receivable/payable. I am not a business person by any means, but I am not willing to outsource those responsibilities yet. I read a lot of books on law practice management and just take things one day at a time."*—Mindy Rush Chipman (class of 2007)

*"Nobody teaches you how to be a owner of a law firm. They generally teach you how to be a research monkey for a firm.* [So, for me I was least prepared for] *abstract examination, office management, payroll, accounting, and how to say 'no' to clients."*—Pat Dillon (class of 2003)

*"It wasn't so much legal skills* [for which I was unprepared], *but rather the skills necessary to run a business. I found I knew how to practice, but running my own business was an eye-opener and required me to learn a whole new skill set."*—John Thrasher (class of 1993)

*"Law school did very little to teach me how to set up my business. It also did very little to prepare me for the process of completing title searches or real estate closings."*—Fred Peet (class of 1993)

*"Although I felt confident about my grasp of the law, I was not as well prepared for the practical details of practicing law. For example, I knew the basic law regarding a home purchase, and I had attended countless CLE sessions about conducting closings, handling real estate transactions, and the like, but I didn't know the specifics of exactly how I should handle sending an abstract to opposing counsel during a real estate purchase. A quick call to other local attorneys helped me solve some of those practice issues, but it's humbling to admit that you can explain the law, but you aren't sure exactly which step comes next in this process when you're just starting out."*—SHAWN SWEEN (CLASS OF 2004)

*"New attorneys know a significant amount of legal knowledge. But how to apply it to practical situations is a real challenge. I suggest you spend time sitting at the courthouse to see how cases actually move. Ask an attorney if you can sit in on a client intake unless you've had experience in these matters. Above all, ask questions! I recall the first time I was asked to sit with a new client and get the information when my employer had an emergency out of the office. I sat at the big desk; the clients came in and sat down. They outlined a problem with a well and water supply. I inquired about all sorts of details regarding what went wrong, how it happened, the identity of all the parties, etc. I prepared a comprehensive summary for my boss, and was ready to move forward when he came in the following morning. He viewed the report and asked me one question: "A dug well or artesian?" I had no idea what he was talking. I had grown up with city water! I had all the law needed, just none of the "common sense" as to who would be responsible and how the problem might be corrected."*—BRUCE DORNER (CLASS OF 1977)

## Q: What are the biggest challenges when you're the boss?

*"How to budget and how to read financial statements. No one should start and run a business who cannot read financial statements. And the next* [challenge] *is in understanding the difference between cash and accrual accounting; you can't eat accounts receivable."*—DEAN N. ALTERMAN (CLASS OF 1989)

*"*[The biggest challenge when you're the boss]? *You're not just the boss… you're the secretary, the IT department, the marketing department, the CPA, and everything else!"*—JENEE OLIVER (CLASS OF 2005)

*"*[As the boss] *you need to establish a budget for insurance (health, dental, malpractice, disability), and any of the other services normally provided by an employer. Second, set up a time management and appointment system, because*

*you will have to wear many different hats on any given day, including collector, lawyer, accountant, PR expert, or janitor. [Having a system in place] helps to ensure that your highest priorities are always addressed. Third, talk to a CPA, and keep an organized file for any records that may be required by the IRS, including business receipts and income statements."*
—Kevin Afghani (class of 2004)

*"[My biggest challenges]? 1) Fees. Deciding how much to charge in fixed fees, and which clients to turn away. I changed my fixed-fees several times until I finally figured out what my time was worth and what my clients could pay. 2) Office administration. I was not familiar with this side of the practice, so I had an accountant teach me how software could track items for tax purposes. 3) Self-confidence. There are still dry spells in my business, and I have doubts that it will come back. I cope by maintaining the online support networks (primarily Twitter and Solosez), and chatting and listening to other solos going through the same situations."*—Stephanie Kimbro (class of 2003)

*"My biggest frustration was, and still is, the realization that law school did nothing to prepare me for actual practice. I thought for sure that toiling those three years—under constant stress and anxiety—would provide the knowledge I needed to practice law. I am just amazed how precious little I learned about real-life litigation in law school, and that feeling has not waned. I almost admire those graduates who show up to court with improper filings and unfounded arguments because at least they're learning by trial and error."*
—Gina Bongiovi (class of 2007)

*"My biggest frustration as a solo is the same I've had since Day 1: no steady stream of revenue, no regular paycheck, and I never know from one month to the next what will be coming in."*—Marc W. Matheny (class of 1980)

## Q: How did you create a revenue stream in the beginning?

*"Criminal defense. It is like raising hogs on a farm. You may not like it, but the cash flows."*—Pat Dillon (class of 2003)

*"[I] lined up contract work with other larger firms, provided exceptional services to the clients of referral persons, and was lower priced than the competition."*—John Thrasher (class of 1993)

"When I graduated, I worked for a local attorney doing primarily real estate titles and closings. In those days all the attorneys worked on the title research at the Registry of Deeds. We all shared information, we all gathered for lunch, and we all supported each other. When the real estate boom ended and I went out on my own, these colleagues sent me their smaller cases, their conflicts, and any overload work. I always accepted the referrals and made it a point to make sure the client was sent back to the referring attorney for any future work."
—BRUCE DORNER (CLASS OF 1977)

"I keep my overhead as low as possible…and I mean LOW. My office rent is $1 per month, I keep the thermostat at 60 degrees, I use my smartphone for my business phone and get Internet off my phone, I use my laptop for my computer and bought most of my office supplies (printer, etc.) on Black Friday for dirt-cheap. I also barter for a lot of my services. For example, my office needed to be cleaned, so I traded cleaning services for legal services."
—MINDY RUSH CHIPMAN (CLASS OF 2007)

### Q: What would you tell new solos about malpractice insurance?

"Buy it. You'll sleep better, and, hopefully, you won't need it. There are so many stressful aspects to running your own business and being a solo practitioner that it just makes sense to take this one off the list and insure this risk."
—CAILIE A. CURRIN (CLASS OF 1988)

"Get it. You've got enough on your mind without worrying about [a malpractice claim]. And [the insurance] probably isn't as expensive as you think for a new attorney, and it will give you real peace of mind."
—MITCHELL J. MATORIN (CLASS OF 1993)

"Absolutely essential. Dealing with the public is unpredictable. Protect yourself at all costs."—ABBE W. MCCLANE (CLASS OF 2003)

"Shop around. Don't allocate more than 5% [of coverage] to any practice area you're not telling people you handle. For example, if you plan to be a family lawyer but might do a few estate plans, give the family law section 95% and the estate planning section 5%. I was told that anything over 5% or 10% triggers a new practice area and increases your premiums. I was also assured that if you are sued for something outside your listed practice areas, you're still covered by the insurance. So don't increase your premiums unnecessarily."
—GINA BONGIOVI (CLASS OF 2007)

*"Buy it. Just don't buy more than you need. Above all, watch carefully, take your time, and the need to notify your carrier will be reduced."*
—Bruce L. Dorner (class of 1977)

*"Research, research, research! Make sure you understand the provisions of the policy and the coverage. Pay attention to indemnification clauses; whether the provider can settle without your consent; whether you can choose your own defense counsel; and the amount of coverage for each claim and the aggregate coverage."*—Adam Neufer (class of 2009)

*"The decision as to whether to purchase malpractice insurance depends heavily on your State Bar rules and the clients you intend to serve. Speaking for myself, I waited to get malpractice insurance until I felt it was necessary. In particular, I was talking to potential clients that required me to have malpractice insurance. In that situation, I felt it was worth the investment."*
—Kevin Afghani (class of 2004)

*"If you unbundle legal services or use technology in your practice, understand what is and is not covered in the malpractice policy regarding coverage of hardward and software. Educate your carrier about what you are using and discuss it with them."*—Stephanie Kimbro (class of 2003)

*"It really depends on your practice area and who your clients are. I flew without anything in my first16 months of practice. Doing mostly transactional work and working mostly with people I had known before, I didn't feel too exposed. I put it off until the middle of my second year. In the end, the online solo community helped me to make my decision on how much and with whom to insure."*—Jan M. Tamanini (class of 1984)

### Q: How important is a business plan?

*"[A business plan] is extremely important. It provides you with a solid goal and a plan on how to achieve it. And then it projects past the goal to a greater one."*—Abbe W. McClane (class of 2003)

*"A business plan is critical because it forces you to think about the type of practice you hope to establish, and it gives you insight into challenges and competition. With a business plan, you will feel that you are better able to make informed decisions about your practice."*—Tonya Coles (class of 2006)

"Business plans are important, but they don't have to be 50 pages long. [Mine was] a mission-and-vision statement, with a budget, some goals, and the names of everyone I would contact about referrals. That was about it."
—Michael Moebes (class of 2003)

"A business plan is of the utmost importance. I don't see how [a solo can succeed] without one. It doesn't have to be super-formal. Just a basic budget; things like how much expenditures you will be making each month, how much money you need to cover those expenses, how much you need to cover overhead, and to bring home a decent salary."—Paul Scott (class of 2008)

"I kept my business plan pretty simple, and continue to develop it to this day. To me, a business plan should be a growing organism that takes account of your expanding knowledge and experience base. Sometimes, the simple act of committing your plans to writing can help to ensure that you follow through on those plans. Of course, a business plan is only as effective as your willingness to stick to it. Therefore, merely making a plan is only the first step in starting your law firm, and will do nothing by itself."—Kevin Afghani (class of 2004)

"I worked for two years on my business plan before I opened my practice, and I am very glad I did. Without it, I think it would have taken four to six months to turn a profit; with the plan, I made a profit within two months after opening and in every month since."—Dean N. Alterman (class of 1989)

"I think it's very important for me to put things on paper. Frankly, I haven't followed most of what I wrote in my first business plan, but it was a really useful exercise. And the financial part of it is incredibly important so you can budget if things don't take off for a while."—Matthew G. Kaiser (class of 2002)

"Whether you draft a traditional, formal business plan, or spend just a few pages outlining your goals and expectations, you really should have some plan in place…and review it and update it regularly (say, every six months). Without one, it would be like driving across country without a map. Sure, you may eventually get to your destination, but it won't be by the most direct or effective route."—Jan M. Tamanini (class of 1984)

"It certainly makes life easier to know where you are going, so you'll know when you get there. Setting reasonable goals and monitoring progress for yourself gives you a chance to see how your practice evolves, and gives you the *opportunity to sit back, reflect, and determine if opportunities exist in other practice areas which might be a good fit for your personality and comfort zone."*—Bruce L. Dorner (class of 1977)

*"It is critical to have a business plan, but also to keep it updated. Your plans for your practice will change as you get more into it, so you have to keep your business plan fluid and refer back to it. It's a document for you to lay out your plans and goals. Take it to a small business center or SCORE office and have them give you feedback on it. It can't hurt."*—Stephanie Kimbro (class of 2003)

*"I think a business plan is crucial. It keeps you on track, and is a great tool to make decisions efficiently. A friend who owns an ad agency explained the best use of a business plan: when you're making a decision about your business, see if* [the decision] *would complement or hinder your company's purpose as outlined in your business plan. If* [the decision] *hinders it, don't do it."*
—Gina Bongiovi (class of 2007)

*"I don't think a traditional, written-out business plan is too important. But you should certainly have a clear idea of what you want, and how you are going to do it.* [Before I began], *a few people grilled me about business and financial projections. But the truth is you can't really project what business might be like in the beginning. So, for certain aspects of going solo, it's more about adaptation than planning."*—Adam Neufer (class of 2009)

*"I don't think* [a business plan] *is very important. Sure, you should take pen to paper and get a general sense of what it will cost to open your doors, how much income you need to bring in, how soon you need income, etc. As a new solo, your business plan can be as simple as this: spend as little as you can, do everything you can do to market your business, and do a good job. That's the plan. If you do those things, you've done what you can to succeed."*
—Mark Tanney (class of 1998)

*"I didn't do one. I know you are supposed to, but I didn't. And I haven't missed it."*—Lynda L. Hinkle (class of 2009)

*"Whether or not to write a business plan probably depends on experience level and practice area. For me, it was not important at all. At least, I didn't have one, and I wouldn't know how to write one. It's possible, though, that I might be vastly more wealthy and nearing financial security if I had had one. I guess ignorance is bliss."*—Mitchell J. Matorin (class of 1993)

"I didn't create a formal business plan before beginning. But several months ago, I did make a marketing plan for the year. It's been VERY helpful in keeping me motivated about marketing."—SARAH WHITE (CLASS OF 2002)

"I started [my practice] without a business plan, and I think I was held back because of it."—MARC W. MATHENY (CLASS OF 1980)

## Q: How do you market a small town practice?

"Never give up. Remember, you're only one phone call away from a great month! As always, don't spend it before you have it in the bank. And, when you've had a really good month, set aside a large chunk in a "rainy day fund" to carry you through the slow times. I've never borrowed money from the bank to keep my office afloat. When I landed a few larger cases I put the money aside and drew on it when the economy went south. It was one of the best business decisions I ever made."—BRUCE DORNER (CLASS OF 1977)

"Word of mouth and small community-based advertising & donations are the best marketing."—JOHN THRASHER (CLASS OF 1993)

"What works? Want ads, a monthly column in the local newspaper, ads at the local movie theater, and a Web site with content. What doesn't work? Legal referral systems that you pay for, and Yellow Pages ads. [Phone book advertising] is for clients who [already] know you but who forgot your phone number."—PAT DILLON (CLASS OF 2003)

"Advertise, go to every social function, send holiday cards, make sure everyone knows what you do, and court those who can refer a lot of business."
—FRED PEET (CLASS OF 1993)

## Q: How do you grow your practice?

"Be responsive, complete your work faster than the competition, give good service, return phone calls and email immediately, be competitively priced, and consider flat-fee pricing."—FRED PEET (CLASS OF 1993)

"Stick to your core areas. Do not provide a true general practice; those days are gone. You can practice in a number of areas, but just don't try to practice in them all. We do not handle family law, criminal law, or bankruptcy. They can be lucrative, but they are not areas that we want to proactive in, and therefore do not dabble in them by only taking one or two cases because those one or two cases will suck your resources as you try to learn the law and the unwritten procedure and protocol in those practice areas."—JOHN THRASHER (CLASS OF 1993)

*"Whether you get involved through religious organizations, charitable groups, or community service, positive name recognition is critical. Offer to write short articles for the local free paper, and see if the local cable TV station would like a few segments about new legal issues."*—Bruce Dorner (class of 1977)

*"How do you grow your practice?* [By] *adding value to clients and showing them that you are increasing their wealth, happiness, or bottom line. Also, by asking other lawyers for work. You get what they don't want."*
—Pat Dillon (class of 2003)

## Q: What did your most challenging clients teach you?

*"Some clients want to run the show and tell you how to handle the case.* [Other] *clients tell you that a lawyer friend told them you should handle the case in a particular fashion. When I hear that I say, 'Let's get the friend (or lawyer) on the phone to discuss the situation.' Nine times out of ten, the friend or other lawyer is a myth. In the one out of ten times, I enjoy the conversation as I may learn something, or at least rule out that solution since the friend or attorney didn't have all the facts.* [In my experience], *the clients for whom you do the most generally are the least appreciative.* [Suggest] *you bill promptly, as the more time that passes the less the client thinks they needed your services, or that they could have done it themselves."*—Bruce Dorner (class of 1977)

*"*[What's the most challenging]*? Not being able to help folks who were already so far along the path before they decided to get an attorney involved that there was nothing I could do to help the client out of the particular situation. The lesson I learned is that despite your efforts, it can sometimes be too little too late and/or despite pleas for help."*—John Thrasher (class of 1993)

*"There is the 'Sore Loser' loser client who doesn't like the deal achieved for him after we have inked the deal.* [Now] *I make sure I have a full disclosure of all the ramifications in writing before a client signs off on a deal.* [Then there is] *the client who asks for special concessions like late night appointments, Saturday night appointments, or other favors. They're likely to be the first to complain when everything doesn't go their way. The answer: don't give special concessions. If the client values you enough, they won't ask for 'em."*
—Pat Dillon (class of 2003)

# SECTION IV. YOUR NEW LAW PRACTICE

## CHAPTER 19

## Should You Buy a Practice?

*"Surgeons don't operate on themselves, and lawyers should not take themselves as clients. If you're thinking about buying a practice, hire outside counsel or some other disinterested party to act as a reality check, and to knock holes in your grand scheme."*—B. CAMERON

This is not an area where you want to rush in uninformed.

I know, you're a lawyer and you're perfectly capable of handling high-powered commercial transactions in your sleep, and you should have no problem with the simple matter of buying a law practice. Hire outside counsel anyway. Surgeons don't operate on themselves, and lawyers should not take themselves on as clients. At the very least, find some disinterested party to act as a reality check. Ask them to knock holes in your grand scheme, and to ask the questions that will get you to double- and triple-check your due diligence.

If you really want all the nitty-gritty details of buying and selling a law practice, check out Ed Poll's popular blog for lawyers: *lawbiz.com*, and Jay Foonberg's *seniorlawyers.org* (click on **Articles** for a short checklist on valuing a law practice).

So, why buy an existing practice? Consider:

- It can take years for a new rural practice to become established and profitable. Buying a practice can be a quick, ethical way to jump-start your small town legal career and become profitable sooner.
- In one stroke, you get a book of clients, name recognition, an office location with which locals are familiar, and all the equipment, furniture, law books, etc., for running a practice.
- The practice may even come with a staff that knows how to work with the local courts and government bureaucracies, AND the seller may even stay on as of counsel for a time to act as in-house mentor and entree to the community.

Not a bad deal. For a few dollars, you get a turn-key practice, a mentor, and a way to allay the typical small town wariness of something new. After all, if the community knows that you are taking over for ol' Bob Smith, and that ol' Bob will be looking over your shoulder while you get your feet on the ground, folks will have a bit more confidence that you will be doing things "the right way" (that is, how ol' Bob did them for the last 30 years), and they will take comfort in knowing that ol' Bob is going to be there to keep those big city notions to a minimum.

Unfortunately, the reality of buying a practice may differ slightly from the hype.

Unless you're one of those fortunate few who have a few hundred thousand dollars stashed away in your sock drawer, buying an existing law practice will add to your debt load and your firm's overhead. And then there is the matter of what to call your new firm. Understandably, you will want to change the name of ol' Bob's firm. The problem is, if the transition happens too quickly, you stand to lose continuity and—more important—a bridge to the community. The ideal transition—which ought to take place over a few years—would be to move from "The Law Offices of Bob Smith" to "The Law Offices of Smith & Jones" to "The Law Offices of Janet Jones".

**What Are You Buying?**

From the seller's point of view, a law firm's value comes from a mix of goodwill, accounts receivable, an existing book of business, and sundry mundane items like equipment and office space.

From the buyer's point of view the only real value lies in having a referral base and possibly a transferable book of business. Goodwill usually follows a lawyer not a firm; accounts receivable only have value if you can collect them (if the previous lawyer couldn't collect, why do you think you can?); equipment is only valuable if you need it and can use it; and any real estate should be handled in a separate transaction.

In very simple terms, a lawyer's book of business arises from his client base; active matters and matters closed long ago. *A transferable book of business consists of those active clients who chose to remain with the firm and accept you as their lawyer, and those closed matters that have long tails*. Estate plans are the best examples of a matter that generates a long tail; eventually those wills need to be probated and some percentage will return to the firm that wrote the will to handle the probate. Short-tailed matters are things like divorce and criminal matters; both pay well when active, but seldom generate repeat business as clients are more likely to either follow a particular lawyer or choose their next lawyer on the basis of price. Buying a practice focused on short-tailed matters means that you are buying into an immediate, but short-lived income stream, whereas buying a practice with long-tailed matters means that you are buying what should be a long-term income source.

☛ **For the buyer, a practice where the book of business is mainly short-tailed matters is not as valuable as a one that offers a long-tailed book.**

Which brings us to the question of value: what is this book of business worth?

The only correct answer is: whatever a willing seller and willing buyer say it is. And a fat lot of good that does for you. Frankly, I'm not sure typical business valuation methods will work well when applied to a law practice. The transferability of a book of business is highly variable, and the market for used law practices is very immature. So, we are left with the old standbys: supply and demand, and urgency. A rural law practice's book of business may be more transferable than a metropolitan book, but that has more to do with scarcity (the "if-you're-the-only-game-in-town" factor). Still, rural clients may take their business elsewhere for any number of reasons from cost to whim.

## Calculating a Purchase Price

So, you've decided to buy a law practice and have done your due diligence. You are familiar with your ethical obligations, you have hired counsel to draft the necessary documents, and you have an idea of the firm's book of business. There seem to be two commonly used methods of figuring a price for a law firm: (a) Multiple-of-Fee Income and (b) Return on Investment.

***The multiple-of-fee income method.*** The value of the firm is determined by calculating the average yearly gross fee income of the firm over some period (typically, the previous five years) and multiplying it by some number to get to the multiple of fee amount. Typically one uses a starting number of 1.1 or 2.1 as the multiplying factor, and then adjusting that multiplier up or down according to a number of factors. Some adjustment to consider:

**The fee income mix.** Segregate fee income by type ($x from divorce, $y from wills, $z from real estate, etc.), and calculate a five-year average for each type. This will show you how each income type contributes to the firm's overall fee-income. A firm whose majority of income comes from long-tailed matters (income from managing Trusts or that safe full of estate plans), has more value that one whose income is derived primarily from short-tailed matters (those that are as likely to follow the lawyer who generated them as they are to stay with the firm). Adjust the multiplying number up in the former case and down in the latter. While a metropolitan lawyer might consider the source of clients or the growth potential of the firm's practice areas as adjustment factors, the rural lawyer is going to look at other factors: the number of other firms/lawyers in the area, the town's current population, and the growth potential of the region. A high people-to-lawyer ratio or good growth potential are factors that adjust the multiplying number upwards.

**How long will the seller stay with the firm?** If the selling lawyer is willing to stay on for six months or so as a mentor, and to introduce you to clients, adjust the multiplier up; if the seller stays for a shorter period (or if the selling lawyer is deceased), you should adjust the multiplier down. If the selling lawyer wants to stay on for more than a year, perhaps you should be considering entering into a partnership and look into business succession planning rather than an outright purchase.

**What is the net income?** Net income generally runs 40 percent to 50 percent of gross income. If it is much lower, the firm is depending on high volume to meet expenses, and if it is *much* higher, the lawyer may be working very long hours, a sure sign that there is a need for additional staff or resources. Either way, you are going to want to lower that multiplier. You can bump the multiplier up if the seller is willing to guarantee a certain level of income, but expect to negotiate how the selling price and terms should change if the actual income is either over or under the guaranteed amount at certain time points after the sale (say at one and two years post-sale). A guarantee would work in the following manner: payment of the selling price would be spread over some period—say, three years. One- third of the selling price is paid up-front, one-third is paid at the beginning of Year 2, and the balance in Year 3. However, if the net income for Year 1 is less than 90 percent of the average net income seen by the seller, than the amount due in year 2 is reduced by some percentage (e.g., a 5% reduction for every 10% below that 90 percent mark). Similarly, if the net income is greater than 110% of the average net than the amount due in Year 2 is increased by some percentage. The amount in Year 3 could be adjusted in a similar fashion based on the firm's performance in Year 2.

☛ **Be sure you know what you are buying, and consider structuring the deal so you have some protection if your actual income does not match up with ol' Bob's projections.**

**Physical assets.** Office furniture, computers, books, etc., that are owned (not leased) have some value, but don't adjust the multiplier. Simply add their fair market price to the multiple-of-fee amount. Other things that are added are pending, active matters with partially earned fees (provided the client wishes to stay with the firm), and matters being done on a contingency basis (if it is ethically possible to divide those fees). Leased assets are more of a liability than a positive. They tie you into equipment that might not fit your needs and limit your ability to move to newer more efficient technology.

**The return-on-investment method.** You start by determining the average yearly net profits of the firm over the last five years (net profit is gross income less expenses including salaries). Then calculate the amount of money you would have to invest in an alternative investment to generate a similar return. For example, suppose the law firm has net earnings of $75,000, and there is a "no-risk" investment out there that pays five percent. You would have to invest $1.5 million to get a return of $75,000 ($1.5 million at 5% = $75,000). Thus, you can assume that the law firm has a value somewhere in the neighborhood of $1.5 million. But a law firm is not a "no-risk" investment, so you want to adjust that capitalization figure (that five percent return in the example above) to reflect the amount of risk. Generally, capitalization factors used in small business valuation range from 10 percent to 50 percent. You can judge the risk of a law firm by using the same factors you'd consider in computing a multiplier for a multiple-of-fee amount. Any factor that would increase that multiplier will reduce risk and thus reduce the capitalization factor. So, let's say you've determined that you'll use 20 percent capitalization factor because the law firm is relatively low risk, you would compute its value by dividing the net earnings by 20 percent, arriving at a price of $375,000.

**Visit the author's Website at**
**www.RURALLAWYER.com**

## CHAPTER 20

# Hanging Your Shingle

*"Whether you draft a traditional, formal business plan, or spend just a few pages outlining your goals and expectations, you really should have some plan in place…and review it and update it regularly (say, every six months). Without one, it would be like driving across country without a map. Sure, you may eventually get to your destination, but it won't be by the most direct or effective route."*—Jan M. Tamanini (class of 1984)

There are a 1001 things to do when you open your own law office: from buying office furniture to finding an office; from opening bank accounts to getting malpractice insurance; from designing business cards to creating a social networking presence. The good news is that you should be able to put off staffing decisions for awhile. And until you have clients—living, breathing, paying clients—all you really need is a phone and a business plan. Starting your rural practice with a phone and a plan should be good for the short term (say, your first couple of clients or your first six months in practice). But let's look at some of the critical elements in detail:

**Your business plan**. If you do nothing else before you hang your shingle, sketch out a business plan for yourself. Then print it out, keep it on your desk, and review it *regularly*. Don't do what I did: I wrote out a business plan when I first began, then I filed it away on my hard drive, and didn't look at it again for six months! In those six months, my practice had little direction, and my business development efforts were haphazard and ill-defined. I couldn't explain to potential referral sources what my practice was all about when I didn't know myself. I've learned my lesson. Your business plan must be *a living document* with goals for six months, one year, three years, and perhaps as far out as five years…and the plan should be revamped and refined periodically as your goals are met or circumstances change.

***Malpractice insurance.*** There are hundreds of bits of miscellany necessary for a law office, everything from notepads, paperclips, and manila folders to furniture and professional fees. But malpractice insurance isn't one of them. That's because malpractice insurance is a NECESSITY. While there are lawyers out there brave enough to forego malpractice insurance, I'm not one of them. Frankly, I sleep better at night knowing that if I screw up, my malpractice provider has my back. Plus, the company offers me three hours of free ethics and elimination of bias CLE credits a year, it has a great online form library, and they will provide free advice on selecting and running practice management software. (see sidebar box on Page 103).

***Banking.*** It's a good sign if your community has more than one bank; even better if they are part of a state-wide branch (it's the sign of a vibrant, growing community). If this is the case, there is a good chance you will be able to find a reduced-fee business checking account or at least one that allows for free electronic bill pay. Another way to save on your banking costs is to invest in print-your-own-check software. The software takes care of the formatting, and you save half the cost of ordering checks from the bank. While most accounting software will print on pre-printed check stock, VersaCheck provides solutions that interface with accounting applications allowing them to print on completely blank stock. VersaCheck's parent company (G7) offers complete practically plug-and-play check printing solutions that include dedicated printers; something to look into when setting up shop.

As for business banking costs, it is unlikely you will find free business checking (except your trust account). While on the subject of business banking, I should offer a few tips on the care and feeding of your trust account: the importance of keeping your money and your client's money separate has been drilled into you since your first year in law school, and you know that there's no way that you'll ever make that mistake. But here are a couple of simple tips to maintain that steely resolve:

Order your trust account checks in one style and color, and your operating account checks in another style and color. Personally, I prefer red, manual-voucher, middle-check stock for my trust account, and green computer-voucher, top-check stock for my operating account. That way I have to handwrite anything coming out of my trust account, but I can use my accounting software to print regular business checks. My second tip is that you maintain your trust account at a different bank than your operating account. Granted, this assumes that your small town supports two banks, but it does help to prevent accidentally depositing funds into the wrong account.

Remember, co-mingling funds (*even accidentally*) will require a self-report to the State Professional Responsibility Board.

**Keeping the books.** Once you open your doors for business, you'll find that the administrative tasks of running your practice consume more time than you think. I swear that sometime it seems as if I spend 80 percent of my time on administrative tasks and 20 percent of my time actually practicing law. Since you are going to have to do those boring administrative tasks anyway (paying bills, invoicing), why not block out one morning a week to get those annoyances out of the way all at once. And hire an accountant…because you *will* need one before you open your doors. Your accountant should help you pick out accounting software, set up your books and show you how to use your software and, yes, buy the same software your accountant uses. You may hate it, but it will make your accountant's job easier and thus save you money. During your first few years in practice you may only really need to use your accountant's services at tax time, but consider meeting with him/her on a quarterly basis. A quick once-over of your books can help you stay on budget and your accounts in order.

**Utilities.** Just because it's a small or rural community, don't expect low taxes or inexpensive telecom and Internet service. In most small towns, there is a single electrical utility, and a single provider of phone and Internet services. Water and sewer lines might be connected to a municipal utility, but they could just as easily be private affairs (wells and septic systems). Nor can you assume there will be a utility providing natural gas. Bulk liquid propane and heating oil are more common in rural communities. Given the monopolistic nature of things, the only sure way to save on utility costs is to conserve. You'll save money by fixing leaky faucets, and installing those boring little devices such as automatic set-back thermostats and high-efficiency light bulbs. And if you have access to a high-speed Internet line, consider adopting a Web-based telephone service to cut your firm's telecommunications bill in half. You could also try replacing your business phone line with a cell phone. Of course, the problem is that small towns always seem to lie on the fringes of the cell phone coverage map, so try before you buy because the coverage may not be adequate.

**Setting up a virtual law office.** A *virtual law office* is a powerful way for a rural lawyer to leverage technology and overcome one of the great difficulties of rural practice: distance.

Rural clients are often thinly spread over miles of countryside, and even a 30-minute meeting with an attorney can be a half-day affair for the client. But if the client has access to, and a familiarity with the Internet, a web-based virtual law office (VLO) can provide access to legal services without the client losing a half-day's pay. VLO's work best for transactional services (drafting contracts, creating estate planning documents, general document review, or business incorporation), or for limited-scope representations where you are providing a *pro se* litigant the basic guidance and legal advice necessary to navigate the legal system.

In brief, a VLO is a form of customer portal software; that is, a secure, Web-based gateway that lets clients access a specific set of information and services. These days, customer portal software is routinely used for the secure exchange of financial information. For example, if you currently use a bank's online service to pay bills, you are using a customer portal. A VLO will typically add document management, timekeeping, scheduling, and secure client communication to the mix, becoming much more than just any easy way for your clients to pay their bills.

Given the 24/7 availability of the software, a VLO offers you the convenience of working on legal matters outside of traditional business hours. At the same time, the technology offers personalized communications with your clients through individual home pages, online forms, calendars, messaging, and other features. All of which can be far more secure than the simple unencrypted e-mail most lawyers use for electronic communication.

The downside is that VLO technology is still quite new, and there are no firm ethical guidelines or best practices for its use. As we go to press, the ABA's eLawyering Task Force is working on guidelines for virtual law office practice, and there is a small consortium of legal cloud-computing providers working on a set of standards for the profession. But it is already clear that virtual law offices are at the cutting edge of law practice management, and they hold great promise for reducing overhead, improving client communication, and increasing geographic presence. Before you jump into a VLO, though, there is some due diligence required:

- Check with your state's ethics board for their position on VLO's
- Limited scope representation (aka unbundled legal services)
- The necessity of having a physical, brick and mortar office
- The use of cloud-computing software, the use of client portals, and virtual law office technology, and the remote storage of client data.
- Read Stephanie Kimbro's *Virtual Law Practice: How to Deliver Legal Services Online* (ABA, 2011). For the latest information, check Ms. Kimbro's blog at *virtuallawpractice.org*.

A VLO can be a powerful tool or expensive overhead. The only way to be sure that one will fit your rural practice is to gather information beyond the VLO provider's marketing material.

## Some Brick-and-Mortar Basics

As I mentioned earlier, starting a rural practice with nothing more than a phone and a business plan is OK for the short term. Eventually—that is, when meeting clients at their place of work, their homes or in borrowed office space becomes a burden—you'll want to start projecting the image of the "serious lawyer", and that means having an office...whether it's a storefront in the center of town or a spare room in your house.

The availability (and affordability) of office space is highly dependent on the small town you pick. Some small towns are simply too small to have much of a downtown or commercial district (in my case, "downtown" is just three blocks long), and in other places office space may be at a premium because the town supports a vibrant, active, and growing business community. So, the entrepreneurial rural lawyer must think outside-the-box when it comes to office space. For example, perhaps that small one-bedroom house behind the bank would do, or that apartment under the hardware store that fronts the alley. In short, finding office space in a small town will require careful shopping and the occasional bit of serendipity. And while making your selection, remember the realtor's mantra: *location, location, location*. In your case, you want an address that is easy to get to. If it takes more that about four steps to direct a prospective client to your office, or if you have to direct a prospective client around a maze of one-way streets, you might want to reconsider your choice.

Working with a realtor or property management company should be one of the first stops in your search for office space...but not your only stop. You are just as likely to find an office by reaching out and talking to local business people. Not just the business people already working downtown, but also the guy running the gas station at the edge of town, who might be related to someone looking for someone to rent a two-room office.

***Your first office.*** Your office should fit your immediate needs and not your future plans. So, before you go shopping, have some idea of the amount of space you'll need, how much rent you'd like to pay, and the importance of signage and frontage (the space in the back of a building is often less cheaper than that along the street). If you are starting out as a staff-less solo, you shouldn't need more than about 500 square feet of space. That should allow room for a private office (125 sq. ft.), a meeting room for six (150 sq. ft.), and a waiting area (125 sq. ft.), with a little left over for halls and walls. If you are fortunate enough to have an assistant, look for something with about 625 sq. ft. Of course, until you have clients—living, breathing, paying clients—all you really need is a phone and a plan. With a phone, you can get business cards, you can start marketing your practice, and your potential clients can get hold of you. Of course, once you do have client(s), it's time to buy the most laptop you can afford, invest in malpractice insurance, and open your bank and trust accounts. Later, when you have a dozen clients, you should also invest in a practice-management system.

**Don't rule out buying.** If you are planning on buying a house and renting office space, why not consider that building with a couple of street-level shops and three second-story apartments? Having a place to live, an office, and a potential secondary income stream might not be such a bad thing. Sure, apartment living has its disadvantages and being a landlord can be a hassle. But even if the rental income does nothing more than cover your mortgage payments, that's money your practice doesn't have to supply; besides you can always move into that house once your practice is a going concern. Owning means you can renovate, and renovation, especially if visible and public, is a newsworthy event in a small town. So, if you are the least bit handy around tools, sweat-equity is your friend.

> *"Before I opened my practice, I bought a downtown Main Street building, and renovated it very publicly. I invited the local newspapers to report on our progress throughout the process. By the time I opened, people in most of the surrounding communities knew that I was be opening up and had been following our progress. The historic renovation occurred in a very visible location and people spent a full year peeking in the windows of my building."*
> —SHAWN SWEEN (CLASS OF 2004)

**Office furniture.** When it comes to office furniture, buy quality (it looks more professional and lasts longer). Does that mean you have to buy new? No. Estate sales, governmental surplus sales, and office equipment auctions are great places to find quality pieces at reasonable prices. And the good news is that you won't need much right away. Think "functional" when it comes to your work space; a desk, a couple of chairs, a good desk lamp, and a small filing cabinet is sufficient. There's no need for coordinated colors or matching styles. In time, of course, you'll need to set up a meeting room with a table and chairs for six. And still later, when you're scheduling back-to-back meetings with clients, you'll need a waiting area that has an end table or two, and seating for between four and six. A note about waiting room decor: those plush Italian leather sofas may look great but may be inappropriate, especially if it takes an elderly client or prospective client 15 minutes just to get on their feet. Remember, their comfort comes first.

***A few words about leasing.*** Leasing office equipment is a mixed blessing. On the one hand, you can get all that really great, high-end electronics, and it may give you a tax break. On the other hand it only adds to your overhead, and for the average rural firm, overhead can make or break profit margins. With the exception of office space, the motto of the newly-arrived rural lawyer should be pay cash or do with out because having a minimalist bottom line will put you on the fast-track to a profitable practice. Besides, a startup practice really does not need a work-group class copier or vast expanses of Steelcase furniture. Eventually, your firm will grow to a point where leasing may make sense. When that moment in time occurs, it will be between you and your accountant.

## Office Equipment Basics

Unless you are fortunate enough to be joining an existing firm, you need to invest in all the supplies that support a law office. Where possible, buy locally. Business cards, for example. Everyone knows you can save a bundle by ordering business cards from online printers, but will your online printer send you clients the way your local printer might? I don't think so.

The thing about office technology is you should invest in technology you actually need, not the gadgets you want. And always evaluate technology in terms of functional life-span (obsolescence), total cost over that life-span, future-proofing, and return on investment.

The sole purpose of office technology should be to improve your efficiency because efficiency is your friend, it keeps you focused, and focus yields better outcomes. But if that pretty little piece of silicon won't add to your revenue stream, think twice before buying it. In this economy, clients are interested in one thing and one thing only: outcomes. They are interested in paying for solutions to their problem. So, your office technology must have a positive impact on outcomes. And for each product or service, ask yourself, "*What difference will it make*?" If you can't answer the question truthfully, the technology is probably unnecessary.

I'm going to assume that you are outfitting your office from scratch, and will be looking for the minimal technology to get you through the first few years of your practice. So, with that caveat, here's my recommended shopping list:

- **A laptop.** Unless you truly enjoy being tied to your office, you'll want a laptop rather than a desktop computer. Recent advances have brought desktop-replacement computing power to commercial-grade laptops, and there is little price difference now between commercial- and consumer-grade systems. When it comes to laptops, there are three go-to systems: the Lenovo ThinkPad series, the Apple Macbook Pro series, and the Apple Macbook Air. And of the three, Apple's Air is, in my opinion, the best of the bunch. It's a three-pound *wunderkind* of a computer with an eminently useable keyboard and enough computing power to give most desktops a run for their money. For comfortable desktop use, you can plug the Air into Apple's 27-inch Thunderbolt display, and have a system that can display two letter-size pages side-by-side. And the Air happily runs Windows and Linux, so you don't have to be tied to Apple's way of doing things. No matter which laptop you buy, be sure to outfit the system with as much RAM as it can hold (RAM is the cheapest way to improve performance and future-proof a computer), and get the largest external monitor you can afford (you'll be doing your eyes a favor).

- **A printer.** Don't buy a multifunction printer/copier/fax/scanner/espresso machine. They're disasters-in-waiting because a single malfunctioning component can take down the whole system and leave you with a nonfunctioning paperweight. Instead, buy a good color laser printer capable of duplex printing and a document scanner. What you want is a fast (15 to 25 pages per minute) printer that supports multiple paper trays, will print on both sides of a page (duplex), will print envelopes, and is capable of printing 750 to 2,000 pages/month. Inkjet printers? I'm not a fan of them. They're inexpensive (you may even get one for free when you purchase your laptop), but their replacement ink cartridges often cost as much as the printer itself.

- **A document scanner.** For now, the best bargain out there is Fujitsu's ScanSnap series. They are drop-dead-press-one-button-simple to operate. They automatically scan both sides of the document in color and output a PDF file. And you can often find ScanSnaps bundled with a copy of Adobe Acrobat. The only problem is that ScanSnap scanners are not TWAIN-compliant, and they do not play well in a Linux environment or with software that is not compatible with their proprietary drivers. If ScanSnaps aren't for you, look for a scanner capable of duplex scanning, scans in color, and has a sheet-feeder capable of handling at least 25 sheets of paper. At a minimum, you want a scanner that can scan both letter and legal size sheets, but it's best to find one that can handle everything from business cards to ledger size (11"x 17").

- **An external disk drive.** You'll need some place to archive your system backups (actually, you'll want two places; one in your office and one outside). For Apple users, the best option is Apple's 2 TB Time Capsule. The Time Capsule works in concert with Apple's Time Machine (part of the MacOS) backup software to automatically and wirelessly backup your system. It is about as close to a plug-in-turn-on-and-forget system as you can get. As a bonus, the Time Capsule acts as a router and print/disk server, reducing the amount of equipment you have to buy, and making its price a bit easier to swallow. Otherwise, the Western Digital 2 TB My Book Essential is a cost-effective alternative that comes bundled with its own backup software. By the way, if you don't think you need to have a backup system, think again. Two percent of all desktop computers and 10 percent of all laptops will experience a data loss event in any given year[1], and 60 percent of businesses that lose their data close their doors within six months of the loss![2] Think of backup systems as an insurance policy; you hope you'll never need them, but you'll be glad you have it that morning when everything goes south (see Chapter 21 for more on data storage).

- **A router.** Routers are unnecessary until you have more than one computer (although I happen to like the extra security I get by placing a router between my computer and the rest of the Internet). Shopping for routers isn't complicated. Get one with at least four ports, and supports WiFi (802.11n) and gigabit Ethernet. Both Apple's Airport Extreme (if you didn't get the Time Capsule), or Cisco's small business line of routers like the WRVS4400N, are reliable choices.

- **Copy machine, fax machine.** You don't need a copy machine (scanner + printer = copy machine), nor do you need a fax machine (scanner + eFax service or scanner + fax modem = fax machine). Just get in the habit of scanning every document that comes into your office. Give the original to your client and store your copy electronically. Digital information is cheaper to store than paper file folders, file cabinets, and the reams of paper you'll need for those hard copy files. If that big, once-in-a-blue-moon copy job crops up, just download the documents to a flash drive and head over to the local copy center and let them print them for you. This is cheaper than maintaining a fussy copy machine, AND it gives you an opportunity to network with a local business.

- **Word processing software.** There is really only one choice: Microsoft Word, the industry standard. While there is better word processing software (e.g., LibreOffice, Apple's Pages, Google Docs), Word is the 800-pound gorilla as it applies to page layout, typography, and collaboration. So, if you don't want to go through the hassles of importing Word documents into an alternate format, and then exporting from that format into Word, just give in to the inevitable right from the start. Note: don't buy Word alone, get a copy of Office; you'll eventually use the other bundled applications.

- **A contact/calendar/e-mail system.** Again, the industry standard is Microsoft Outlook (and if you have Office, you have Outlook, so there is nothing more to buy). If you are going to use Outlook, also get yourself copy of Xobni (a free contact management system for Outlook). Xnobni provides better contact tracking, better threading (what was the last e-mail I sent to this contact), and better searching than Outlook. I would also recommend using a hosted exchange-server (Microsoft Office 365 is one of the better bargains at $4–$8 per user per month depending on the service level you choose) rather than trying to manage things though low-level protocols (CalDAV, SMTP, POP, IMAP), or shelling out the bucks for your own in-house exchange server. There are several alternatives to Outlook. The best is Mozilla's Thunderbird/Lightening/Sunbird suite of programs. These three programs are fast, free, and work together seamlessly.

- **Accounting software.** There is really only one go-to piece of software for small business accounting: it's Quickbooks. For accountants, Quickbooks is the industry standard; for non-accountants, it is a horrid piece of software. Yes, there are alternatives, including GnuCash, which is free and much more user-friendly. But the trade-off is that you'll have to spend time importing and exporting data when your accountant goes over your books later. This has to be done very carefully as GnuCash lacks Quickbook's "accountant's copy" feature, and does not automatically reconcile any changes your accountant may have made. While I loathe Quickbooks, this was one instance where experimenting with alternatives was going to cost me more money than simply buying Quickbooks. I should note that some of the best money I've ever spent was the $100 I spent having my accountant teach me how to set up my books, and how to use the half-dozen Quickbooks functions I would need regularly.

- **A practice-management system.** There are two schools of thought when it comes to practice management software: "roll-your-own" and "buy-integrated". The "roll-your-own" school says that you can pull together your own functional system from a set of assorted, no cost/low cost task list-and-tickler applications, including Google Calendar (calendar stuff), Gmail (e-mail & contact management), FreshBooks (time tracking), MyFax (faxing), EchoSign (e-signatures on documents). By creating your own solution, you can use tools that work the way you practice, and you have the flexibility to adopt new technology as it develops. Having your own solution means that you can quickly adapt to changes in your practice.

  The "buy-integrated" school believes that there is value in having a flexible, integrated, single software solution if for no other reason than to eliminate the need for repetitive data entry. Juggling data across multiple pieces of software takes time that you could otherwise spend on lawyering. The argument for using a unified, integrated solution is this: easier is better than harder, simple is better than complicated, integrated is better than separate, a single entry is better than multiple entries, looking in one place is better than having to look in several places, and it is easier to get support from one competent company than from several companies (each of whom will blame the others).

  I fall into the "buy-integrated" camp (if I were to roll my own, I'd spend more time tweaking the software than I would spend lawyering; not a profitable way to a practice). Frankly, you won't go wrong by using any of the first-tier, unified practice management solutions. The key is to find one that works for you and most, if not all, of the first-tier products offer some type of try-before-buy option. Among the first-tier practice management solutions are Amicus Attorney, TimeMatters, Prolaw, PracticeMaster/Tabs3, Clio, RocketMatter, MyCase, Advologix, and Credenza Pro. If you are cost-conscious and willing to take a little risk on an "up-and-comer" you might also consider TotalAttorneys, REDIoffice, Daylite, or HoudiniEsq. If you are a solo and have yet to invest in a practice management system, do give HoudiniEsq a hard look. It's free, it syncs with Word, Outlook, Excel, and Quickbooks, it offers document management, document assembly, and a Web-based client portal. If you don't like HoudiniEsq, you can export your data as .csv files, a file format that is readable by most other practice management systems.

## MALPRACTICE INSURANCE? GET IT, YOU'LL SLEEP BETTER

There are three basic reasons to buy malpractice insurance:

1. *To protect your income stream*: defending a malpractice suit can be a long, expensive drain on your finances.
2. *To protect your clients*: let's be honest, occasionally an attorney is negligent and that negligence can cause damage to a client. So as a matter of public policy, if not simple professionalism, a lawyer should avoid leaving a client unprotected.
3. *To protect you and your family's assets*: a single malpractice judgment can easily wipe out years of work spent building personal wealth.

Current data (based on the 2008 and 2012 ABA Malpractice surveys) shows that, on average, a lawyer can expect three malpractice claims over the course of a career, with mid-career attorneys (11–20 years of experience) seeing the brunt of those claims (especially those with real estate, family law, or personal injury practices). There does not seem to be a difference in malpractice rates between rural and metropolitan lawyers; it seems we are all equally human and equally prone to making mistakes. When buying malpractice insurance, the general rule of thumb is to buy enough coverage so that you will be covered for two claims per year. Given that I can imagine a claim might really big numbers, I've always taken this to mean: buy as much coverage as you can afford. But no matter how much coverage you buy, be proactive and do everything you can to avoid a claim.

The ABA provides the following 10 tips to avoiding a malpractice claim:

- *Don't be afraid to turn down a client.* Trust your gut; if the client or the matter doesn't feel right, don't take it
- *Don't forget your small cases.* Stay in regular contact with all your clients. Reviewing all your cases on a weekly basis will help keep you from overlooking that small matter that's sitting at the bottom of the pile.
- *Use a retention agreement.* Your retention agreement should do more than set out your fee schedule, evergreen clause and dispute resolution mechanism. It should also state the scope of your representation in clear, unambiguous terms.
- *Manage client expectations.* The average, first-time client expects the legal system to work the way it does on TV; trials never last longer than 60 minutes, the good guys always prevail, and lawyers seldom send out bills. As their counselor, part of your job is to educate them on the in's and out's and intricacies of the legal system, its delays, expenses, and unpredictable outcomes.

- *Return phone calls.* For that matter, return emails, letters, postcards, and any other communications from the client promptly. Let your clients know your policy for returning phones calls and stick to it. There is nothing like unreturned communications for turning happy clients into unhappy ones.
- *Don't sit on your mistakes.* Mistakes don't go away on their own. If you make a mistake, don't try to hide it; get some objective advice from someone you trust, fix it if you can, tell your client, and let your malpractice provider know.
- *Think twice before you sue to collect unpaid fees.* Suing a (former) client is a gold-plated invitation to a counter-claim of malpractice, so think very carefully before opening this particular can of worms.
- *Be diligent in billing and collecting fees.* There are several good reasons for billing on a regular periodic basis. It provides an opportunity to stay in regular contact with the client (don't just send a bill, send a bill and an update letter), it allows you to review all of your active files regularly, and it keeps the cash flowing into your practice. Plus it allows you to monitor those accounts that are consistently past due, and gives you the opportunity to fire the client before you get into a position where you are working for free because you are no longer able to withdraw without prejudice.
- *Write it in your calendar then write it in a back-up calendar.* Missed deadlines are the Number one cause of malpractice claims. So if a matter has a deadline, or is time/date-related, put it in your calendar and then put it in a back-up calendar because you never know when you might lose the first one. Oh, and don't rely on automatic mechanisms to keep your calendars in sync; review them on a daily basis (Google calendar and Outlook may play well together today, but remember you are only one update from catastrophe).
- *Look for conflicts.* Be very proactive in your conflict-checking. Most potential or actual conflicts can be easily foreseen, and many can be resolved, at the start of a matter with a simple inquiry and a waiver of conflict letter, both of which are far less costly and embarrassing than a malpractice claim.

Finally, some of the biggest malpractice risk factors are depression, alcoholism, drug addiction, and job stress. If you are having issues with chemical dependency or mental health please get help; there are organizations (like Lawyers Concerned for Lawyers) that provide confidential support to attorneys for a variety of mental or chemical health issues. Don't be afraid to ask for help; being stoic simply leads to ulcers and potential malpractice claims.

## CHAPTER 21

# High Tech in a Rural Setting

*"Small towns are places where the local ISP still offers dial-up connections and a fast Internet connection is a DSL running a 125 kbps up-link and 1 Mbps down. The good news is that the situation is improving."*—B. CAMERON

Technology comes slowly to rural communities.

In the early 1930's, almost all urban and metropolitan homes had electricity while only 10 percent of rural homes were electrified. It would take another 40 years and the Rural Electrification Administration (once a division of the US Department of Agriculture) before the vast majority of rural homes would have electrical and telephone service. A similar situation exists today with respect to the essentials of modern connectivity: cell phones and broadband Internet. Small towns are places where the local ISP *still* offers dial-up connections and a fast Internet connection is a DSL running a 125 kbps up-link and 1 Mbps down, and where it is still possible to for a cell phone to report an analog signal.

The good news is that the situation is improving

So, what should you expect when it comes to modern telecommunications in a small town? Well, figure that most rural connectivity is somewhere in the computer age's equivalent of the 1950's; Internet connections are available, but they're more expensive, slower, and a bit less reliable than the big city equivalents. You'll find that it is more likely that the local telephone company is also the only practical source for Internet connectivity, and the type and speed of that connection is dependent on the distance between your office and the phone company's switching hardware. The closer you are the more options (and speed) you'll have.

Satellite-based Internet providers are an alternative source of connectivity if your law office has a clear line of sight to the southern horizon (if you can't get satellite TV, you can't get satellite Internet). In my neck of the woods, the cost of satellite Internet is within a dollar or two of the local telephone company's service, and the upload/download speeds are, for all intents and purposes, identical. The only advantages to using the local telephone company is that their repairman lives a couple of miles away and, in all likelihood, the phone company's service will usually work in weather (rain, sleet, snow) that can cause satellite systems to drop signals.

Cell phone service is another piece of technology that is coming slowly to rural areas. Voice service is far more ubiquitous than data, but coverage is nowhere as complete as it is in metropolitan areas. If you think there are holes in your coverage in the big city, then you are going to find great chasms in rural areas. Indeed, the further your town is from major highways, or the more it is isolated by those picturesque hills, valleys, mountains, forests, lakes, etc., the less likely that you will have anything approaching adequate cellular service. Despite all the coverage charts and marketing promises, in many places only one provider will have anything approaching reasonable service. The best way to find a good cellular provider, and before you sign a contact, is to ask the locals which provider they use. But remember, even with "good" cellular service, don't expect to use your cell phone as a substitute for a landline.

### Cloud Computing in a Rural Setting

As you know, the concept behind cloud computing is that you don't have to hire an IT professional, or pay for—or maintain—a server or software! Your service provider does it all for you. They keep the software up-to-date, and their newest features automatically appear. Moreover, the software is available 24/7 from anywhere you can access the Internet, and from any device that can run a web browser. From a user's point of view, cloud-based storage acts like just another disk drive, and is practically invisible, often only appearing as a small icon in your system tray. Yet despite its ease of use and its low initial cost (some systems are even free), I'm personally not a fan of cloud computing. I'd rather have my data and my backups sitting on hard drives that I can actually touch rather than sitting on a server somewhere in the world, and where service is provided by someone I don't know, and who I most-likely can't prosecute if things go south in a big way.

And then there's the problem with...continuity.

The Internet can be a fragile thing in rural America because access depends on your community's utility providers (electricity, phone, cable, etc.). And if, because of the vagaries of weather or the utility provider's carelessness, your access to the Internet access is disrupted, so is your access to your cloud-stored files and software. In fact, when utility services are disrupted, the rural areas and small towns are the last on the company's fix-it list. After all, it is just common sense to repair service in high-density areas before those areas where a mile of wire may only serve four households.

If you are worried about data protection, use an enterprise-class RAID array (4 TB systems can be found for under $1,000, come with 5-year warranties, and will maintain the integrity of your data even if one of the drives in the array fails catastrophically). If you are concerned about losing an external drive to environmental catastrophe (fire, flood, tornado), use a hardened disk drive like ioSafe. And if you want the additional security of off-site backups, use backup software like Crashplan to create your own private cloud, and use your home computer to provide backup storage for your office machines. If you are also concerned about data theft, use disk encryption software (one of the best encryption programs out there, TrueCrypt, is free) to secure your data as it is being written to your hard drive. Unless the data thief has your encryption key, he won't be able to read your files.

For those rural lawyers whose towns have consistently reliable Internet connectivity, you must also ask yourself: are you going to rent your software or own your software? This is one place where it might be a good idea to talk to your accountant and see if there are any tax advantages for you one way or another. Another thing to consider is whether you want to increase your start-up costs (buying software) or your monthly overhead (renting software).

If you are leaning toward cloud computing, ask one or more service providers some or all of the following questions:

- Is the host's servers, offices, and tech support all located within the US? Note: this is not a plug to "buy American". It's more like, "*If you gotta sue 'em, you want to be able to serve 'em*".
- Does the host store data on their servers or on your hardware? Remember, the Internet is not that 24/7 presence in rural areas as it is in cities. You have to plan for power outages, and for the possibility that if connectivity is lost it could be some time (think days, not hours) before it is restored. If your data is on the provider's server, are you prepared to do without until your Internet connection is restored?

And ask these questions if your data is stored on the provider's servers:

- *If you want to terminate service, how do you get your data out*? Do you have to monitor a long-download process, or will the provider ship your data to you on a DVD? Don't be surprised if the provider charges a fee to burn your data to a DVD and ship it to you.

- *How long do you have to retrieve your data if you terminate the service?* And do they guarantee that your data will be completely destroyed (all copies) when you terminate? Knowing if there is any grace period between when you terminate the service and when the data is destroyed, and whether or not the destruction of all copies is guaranteed, will help you plan a graceful exit. If they can't or won't guarantee destruction, be prepared to replace each of your files on the server with an empty file with the same name, and to pay for a couple of extra months of service to allow these empty files time to propagate through the provider's system. It's not the most efficient way to manage data, but at least you've made a reasonable effort to safeguard your firm's data.
- *If there is a security breach, will the provider indemnify you for your losses?* Think about it, do you really want to be the only one on the hook if a hacker steals your firm's data through no fault of yours.
- *Is your data encrypted?* What type of encryption do they use and how strong is it? Encryption reduces the risk that a data thief will be able to access the stolen data. But as we know from recent media accounts, there is encryption…and then there is encryption. At a minimum, the provider should be using a 128 bit AES encryption algorithm (often referred to as bank-level encryption). Ideally the provider uses 256 bit AES encryption.
- *Is there any chance that your data could be seen by the provider's other customers* (i.e., how is your data segregated from all the other data)? Remember, if that segregation is managed by software, a single bug has the potential to expose your data to the world.
- *Does the provider do penetration testing?* How is it done? Is it done by an outside firm? You need to know how the provider is keeping one step ahead of the hackers, and to have the assurance that the testing is done by an outside firm. Insiders are too close to the product to truly test for all the weak points; they know how the systems are supposed to work, and tend to limit their testing to stay within design specifications. It takes an outside firm banging away at it to find those "we-thought-no-one-would-do-that" weak points.
- *Does the provider encrypt data during transfer* (i.e., when information is being sent between your computer and theirs, is it encrypted)? What type of encryption is used and how strong is it? When it comes to protecting your data, you want everything to be encrypted —stored data, transmitted data, everything—and at the highest level possible.
- *How does the provider prevent insider breaches?* Data is more likely to be exposed to unauthorized persons through simple human error and

carelessness than by the actions of anonymous evil-doers. The important thing to know is how the provider will handle those inevitable, human lapses.

- *Does the provider guarantee availability?* What happens if the provider fails to meet the promised availability? Remember, you are not the only one who can lose connectivity or have a system crash. You should know how the provider intends to handle this inevitable failure and how (or even if) they intend to compensate you when their failure results in your loss of access.
- *Does the software integrate with the other applications you want to use?* Can it import and export data to the applications you commonly use? This is the "does-it-work-and-play-well-with-others" question. You want to be able to get your data into and out of the service easily rather than waste valuable time rekeying it.
- *Will the provider give you a roadmap and a timetable of their planned enhancements?*
- *What happens when you need support?* Can you talk to a real person? How long will it take to get to that real person? Are there on-line tutorials and self-help options?
- *Does the provider offer a free trial and a month to month service contract?* Don't get into a long-term relationship until you are very, very sure that you are comfortable with both the product and the provider. Most free trial periods are long enough for you to properly evaluate the product; however they are usually not long enough to really find all the warts and blemishes.

## How to Evaluate the ROI of Technology

Costs are easy to quantify (e.g., it's the purchase price plus the direct operating costs of, say, toner or ink, electricity consumed, maintenance contracts, etc.). Benefits are a little more nuanced and difficult to calculate. Consider:

- Does the technology help you improve communication with your staff, your clients, your referral network, your vendors, or your suppliers?
- Does the technology help you provide faster, more accurate, less expensive, or more comprehensive services?
- Does the technology allow you to accomplish tasks you couldn't do before, including those you might had to refer out before?

To realize any benefit from a piece of technology, you first need an action plan. The plan should outline (a) how and when you'll get training and

(b) how soon you can fully commit to the new technology, and stop doing things the old way (note: unless you learn how to utilize an item's potential, you'll never see much of an ROI). Once you know what gadgets you actually need, do as much online research as time allows so you can avoid the common, *I-spent-how-much-for-this*??!!! remorse. According to the New York Times, two sites that can help are *TheWirecutter.com* and *Decide.com*. TheWirecutter's independent reviewers do not provide an exhaustive library of product reviews; they just tell you which product is the best in a given category, and each selection is bolstered by a concise, authoritative article that explains how the reviewer came to this conclusion. *Decide.com* is a price-prediction engine that allows you to search for tech products and find out whether one is about to be supplanted by a newer, better model, as well as whether the price is likely to rise or fall.

Only after you've determined what you want to buy (based on functionality, quality, user reviews) should you shop for the best price. And do your price searches based on model number or product number, never by name; vendors often offer multiple variants of a product under the same name. Searching for product number helps avoid "feature confusion", and insures an apples-to-apples comparison. Also, remember to factor in shipping and handling costs (which can be an arm and a leg) and any sales taxes…and don't hesitate to ask for the corporate discount.

And then there are coupons to consider.

It may turn out that your online shop has promotions that could knock an extra buck (or 50) from the price. Finding out if there are coupons takes only a few extra keystrokes. There are plenty of sites that collect online coupons and promotional codes, but one of the larger and more established players in the field is *RetailMeNot.com*. There you can find codes for free shipping, 20 percent off and other discounts, and deals that might otherwise have eluded you.

I also recommend that you not buy consumer-grade technology unless you have a short term need and can afford to throw disposable technology at it, or are looking to provide a benefit (e.g., free WiFi) to your clients inexpensively. Consumer-grade electronics are those that come up first in a sort-by-price search on a manufacturer's Web site, and they are designed with a 12-month useful life (as reflected in the short warranty period). Generally, I expect to get one-to-three years of functionality from consumer-grade hardware before it becomes obsolete. On the other hand, business- or commercial-grade electronics may cost a few hundred dollars more but are designed for a three-to-five-year useful life and can be functional for twice as long. As a general rule of thumb, if the hardware is part of your practice's infrastructure (that stuff you rely on that absolutely has to work every day, every time, 24/7/365), buy business-grade hardware. If it won't affect your daily operations if the equipment decides to pack it in unexpectedly buy consumer grade.

There you have it, the basic law office for the rural solo attorney. Add a few business cards, some letterhead, a box of envelopes, a good desk, and a comfortable chair, and you'll be ready for your first client.

# CHAPTER 22

# In Their Own Words

### Q: What role does risk play in a solo practice?

*"Every day is a risk. Every client is a risk. Every time you walk into court it's a risk. It's all risk, isn't it? What else is there but endless risk? [A solo practice is] not for the faint-hearted."*—LYNDA L. HINKLE (CLASS OF 2009)

*"I feel like I'm gambling every day. The cases and clients I take have to be good because I am putting everything on the line for them. [To be a solo], you have to have a very high risk tolerance, one where you either 'make it or break it.'"*
—BRIAN T. PEDIGO (CLASS OF 2007)

*"Based on my experience, one of the most important personality traits of a solo practitioner is a high tolerance for risk. If you are uncomfortable with not getting paid for over a month or two, and not being able to accurately project your income—at least in the starting phase—you should think seriously about your decision to solo. Indeed, the risk factor is the main force preventing many of my colleagues from breaking out on their own. One of the commonly cited reasons that my friends give me for not going out on their own is that there is no financial bottom as to how low they can be. They're correct, but some solos find this to be a strong source of motivation: when they sense their income is about to hit rock 'bottom', they double their efforts to get back in the black again."*
—KEVIN AFGHANI (CLASS OF 2004)

*"Risk is the ghost over your shoulder. From month to month, you can't rely on a steady income. You don't know if your clients will pay; you don't know if the phone will ring; you don't know if any consultation will turn into a client; you don't know if your particular niche will be eliminated due to some new legislation. Risk is probably the biggest factor in a solo practice. The trick is to figure

*out how to manage it, strategically and emotionally, so that dips don't sideline you, and you don't overspend in the good months."*
—GINA BONGIOVI (CLASS OF 2007)

*"[A solo's] risk isn't that much different from those borne by other practitioners…with one exception: it's all on you. There's no one else to take up the slack if you have a slow period or get sick. And if one of your clients has a crisis demanding big chunks of your time, you can't just let everything else slide. The best way I've found to manage this—and it's still a struggle for me—is to make sure I give myself more time than I think I'll need to complete a client project. If something should take a few days, I'll tell the client I'll get it done in ten days; if it should take a week, I'll tell the client two. That way, if you finish on your original estimate, the client thinks you're wonderful; if you have something else come up, and you take the longer time, the client isn't disappointed."*
—JAN M. TAMANINI (CLASS OF 1984)

*"Risk is a big factor in starting a solo practice, but risk is a factor in almost all decisions in life. The goal should not be to avoid risk, but to understand, mitigate, and manage it. You have to be willing to risk your money, savings, and steady paycheck. But if you make a good business plan, stick to it, and can see how you are going to feed yourself, you are managing that risk. Before I started my solo practice, I spent hours and hours in front of Excel spreadsheets, figuring out how much income I would need for the practice to stay afloat, how much I needed to bring home, etc. I take the same approach with cases that I decide to take, marketing decisions, etc. There is always going to be a risk that you won't get a good return on your investment."*—PAUL SCOTT (CLASS OF 2008)

## Q: Where do you see small town law practices heading in the next decade?

*"There will always be small towns, and there will always be lawyers in small towns. However, the use of the Internet is changing the use of legal services and many people are trying do-it-yourself tools on the Internet. I don't know what the [legal] landscape will look like five years from now. But I do know that the Internet is a valuable tool, and we need to find better ways to use it to serve our clients."*—BRUCE DORNER (CLASS OF 1977)

*"I foresee a lot more electronic filing and consolidation of court services. I see driving to regionalized court houses for litigation and criminal issues. And I think the children of current clients will be choosing lawyers who have email/*

*Facebook/website access over those who can always be found for morning coffee at the cafe. I also foresee a lot of older practices getting shut down or bought out and turned into satellites. I don't think that is good for small town life. Lawyers are leaders. But when they are merely paid office-minders for the partners who live somewhere else, the small town suffers."*—Pat Dillon (class of 2003)

"I don't think the practice of law will disappear from the small town, but it may change. As legal processes become both more sophisticated and more automated, like in the real estate field, I think the small town firm may lose some of its practice areas. The firms will evolve from serving whatever legal problems your neighbors have into firms that specialize in an area of law, and will use technology to communicate and represent clients from a much broader geographic area such as the whole state, region of the country or even larger areas."
—John Thrasher (class of 1993)

"With the advances of technology and the acceptance of virtual services, the practice of law from small towns is becoming more and more equalized with Biglaw. [In my opinion], *clients from the metro areas will see that "small law" can provide the same services as Biglaw, but much more personally and affordably."*—Mindy Rush Chipman (class of 2007)

## Q: Given what you've learned, would you still choose to practice in a rural setting?

"I'd do it again in a heartbeat."—Karen Holman (class of 2009)

"Yes, I would not have it any other way."—Mindy Rush Chipman (class of 2007)

"We are not going to get rich, but we have a great quality of life for ourselves and our children."—John Thrasher (class of 1993)

"I would definitely still choose to practice in a small town. Part of my passion lies in helping to create a vibrant community in my rural area, and my law practice is a piece of that plan. I have no complaints about the type or availability of work in my rural area either. People here have real legal needs. I consider it such a blessing that I am able to do my work in a community that also happens to be exactly where I want to live."—Shawn Sween (class of 2004)

# CHAPTER 23

# In Conclusion

It has been about two and a half decades since I left suburbia to take up residence in rural America. It's been a fantastic ride.

On the whole, the pluses have so far outweighed the minuses. Sure, there are some months I rack up more pro bono work than paying work; there are some days when playing the balancing game between work and life—between building my practice and making money—leaves me with the grand champion of headaches; and there are times when I doubt that my fees will ever be anything but modest. But living here, where I can watch deer feeding in my front lawn, and I have wild turkeys roosting on my back porch, or I get to see a sunset paint the hills and fields in velvet purples and vibrant reds as I head home from the office, it more than makes up for the tough times. I know I'm missing out on seeing a city skyline from a high-rise corner office. At the same time, living and working where I do, I am able to bring a trained mind and unique skill-set to a small community and make a difference.

Let me tell you about that community:

Located about three hours to the north and west of my law office is a small central Minnesota town of about 15,000. The name is not important, just know that it is a prototypical American hometown, where summer afternoons are spent fishing down on the river, and high school football occupies Friday evenings in the fall; where 4-H'ers and student athletes are just as likely to make the newspaper as are politicians and sports professionals. It is home to 27 lawyers spread across 14 solo practices and four law firms (the largest of which boasts five attorneys). The library is still in the original Carnegie building, the major industries are agriculture and manufacturing, the city hall sits in the center of downtown, and one can circumnavigate the town in little over an hour.

On the surface, the town has a healthy number of attorneys, about what one would expect for a town of this size. It would seem that there would be little room here for newcomers. But the fact is, two-thirds of the town's lawyer population is likely to be retiring over the course of the next decade. I ran into one of these looking-to-retire lawyers at a CLE a month or so ago, and got to talking about his future plans. It seems that he was looking for an associate interested in eventually taking over his practice. For the most part, the job description was what you'd expect: the ideal candidate would have some full-time employment experience, but that experience did not necessarily have to be legal experience. Basically, the new associate needed to know how to work well with others and be willing to learn how to do the law thing. *But the key qualification was that the candidate needed to be willing to live in town; not commute from the suburbs, but actually commit to being part of the community.* And it was for this reason the lawyer was associate-shopping solely by word-of-mouth. His reasoning was that any candidate patient enough to look for a small town job through networking would have to really want to practice in a rural area and would not see relocation as a detriment.

My point is that in many of the small places that lie between cities—the so-called "fly-over" country—there are wonderful opportunities for those willing to commit to these communities, and willing to build personal connections to both the community in general and the rural bar.

In my opinion, the very best reason for being a rural lawyer recently appeared at the end of a short obituary for a respected small town lawyer. At the bottom of those few column inches noting his passing was a line that read, "*The Valley News Dispatch will occasionally run obituary stories on notable local residents. They are news items.*" Not just obits, but news items. An important distinction. A rural law practice may never yield the sort of compensation or bar association awards that you might expect from an urban practice, but the small town lawyer earns a different sort of compensation, and earns a different type of recognition…as a result of which their absence is newsworthy!

So, my young lawyer, go and start the type of rural or small town practice that will make your absence…newsworthy. That's a life worth living.

**Visit the author's Website at
www.RURALLAWYER.com**

# APPENDIX 1

# Interview with the Author

*Education:* Hamline University School of Law; Class of 2007
*Resume:* Practicing law for five years; previously, a research scientist
*Solo practice:* five years
*Practice specialty:* Collaborative family law, probate, and real estate work

## Q: Why did you decide to solo?
**A:** Going solo right out of law school, AND practicing in a small rural town, was the last thing I wanted to do. My plan had always been to find an associate position with a firm doing IP work. After all, what firm wouldn't want an experienced software engineer/biomedical researcher-with-multiple-graduate-degrees-turned-lawyer? As it turns out, hiring partners aren't much interested in an over-40, second-career, "night school" lawyer (actually, I took all my classes on the weekends) who graduated from a Tier 3 school. I don't think I ever had an 'Aha!' moment about solo'ing. It was more the result of the inevitable crush of circumstance and situation. Anyway, it took three months to accept the idea that if I wanted to practice it would be OK to be solo, and another five months before I gathered enough information to be comfortable with the idea, and to have the confidence to make the leap.

## Q: What did you know about solo'ing beforehand?
**A:** I had no idea how complex a solo practice is, or that you that most of your time is spent on marketing and managing the business and a minority of time actually practicing law. Nor did I know that being a solo would be the scariest, most exhilarating, dullest, stimulating, stressful, challenging, satisfying thing I ever attempted.

## Q: What are your first memories of hanging your shingle?
**A:** There was an intense rawness to those first days and months. It was a time of second-guessing and feeling at sea along a dangerous coast with the

fear of disastrous calamity mere moments away (actually, it was a bit like Civil Procedure). I do have fond memories of those clients who allowed me to learn and earn on their dime. But my sharpest memories are more internal than external: the feeling of dread when I walked into the office each morning; the elation of that first client; the surprise when I got a referral; the exhilaration that came from getting a positive result for a client; and the contentment of earning that first fee. I also remember learning that being an advocate didn't mean I had to always find a legal solution for client when common sense advice was all that was needed.

### Q: How did your wife feel about you opening a solo practice?

**A:** Without her support, I don't think I would have made it through law school much less have the courage to solo. Besides providing moral and emotional support, she is my unpaid office manager/chief assistant/proofreader/receptionist/billing department/all around 'gal Friday.

### Q: What about the risks associated with solo practice?

**A:** Going solo means spending large amounts of time and money in a venture with no defined return, and with odds that are undefined, unpredictable, and continuously variable! It's an intricate dance with risk…but NOT a gamble. [To manage risk], you need to think strategically, making decisions based on information and a cost/benefit analysis rather than reacting to immediate events. The fact that I could not predict all the possible risk involved in being solo was one of the biggest stumbling blocks I had when deciding to go solo. Now, risk is what makes my solo practice fun, exhilarating, worrisome…and scary at the same time. It's what keeps me sharp and drives me to do my best work.

### Q: How did you build a revenue stream in the beginning?

**A:** I kept working at my old job, going from full-time to part-time. With a second job, I was able to build my practice without worrying about health insurance and retirement benefits. There's a downside to a second job, though: managing two schedules requires judicious use of vacation days, frank communication [with clients], and a great deal of flexibility. A second job also reduced the number of hours I was able to spend developing, marketing, and working at my practice, so my practice grows at a slower rate.

### Q: What were you least prepared for?

**A:** Law school prepared me to take the bar exam, but it did not prepare me for the business of law. I soon found that the fastest way to [learn] how to file a probate or record a deed is to go down to the courthouse, find a clerk in the appropriate office and say, "I'm a new attorney, how should I do/prepare/order/file _____ so that it makes your job easier?" After that, just fill in the blanks...and don't forget to send a note of thanks to the clerk.

## Q: What do you learn from your best/worst clients?

**A:** That I am in the customer service business, and that there are no best/worst clients out there. While there may be situations where I am unable to fulfill all of a client's needs, it is not their fault that I failed to set or define their expectations properly. The upside is that each client presents an opportunity to do better. This is not to say that there aren't difficult clients, clients who need hand-holding, or clients I'd rather not have taken on. The typical client comes to me during times of stress. They are not in a frame of mind where they can operate at their highest, most rational self. The key is to remember that, in most cases, this is not what this client is really like, nor is this behavior intentionally directed at you.

## Q: What have you learned about marketing?

**A:** The more you know about your ideal client, and the more detailed description you have of that ideal client, the more cost-effective your marketing will be. Three suggestions:

a. Tailor your marketing to your ideal client, and don't waste time, effort, or money on marketing methods that will not reach that ideal client. If your ideal client is between 60 and 80 years of age, male, living on a farm, you may not want to spend a great deal of time building up your social media contacts or your web site's SEO because your client is not likely to see them. But if your ideal client is age 25–35, an urban professional working in software design, your online presence will be vitally important.
b. When preparing marketing materials, you need to get across who you are, what you offer, why you should be hired, where you are located, and how to contact you in an efficient manner.
c. Have a uniform look across all your materials (same colors, same type faces, etc.), and a consistent presence. If you take an ad out in the local shopper, keep it going for several weeks, even months. Name recognition takes time and patience.

## Q: Can you solo on a shoestring?

**A:** Yes. You can set up a solo office on a shoestring; you just can't run a solo practice on one. All those articles on the "$10,000 law practice", the "$5,000 law office", and "starting-a-law-practice-a-shoestring" are correct as far as they go. Their flaw? They don't consider what it costs to live AND maintain your practice. [As you prepare to solo], remember you need to factor in rent or mortgage payments, and those pesky bills for food, utilities, telephone, transportation, health insurance, and taxes. On top of that, there are costs for professional marketing, maintaining your license, and advancing court costs or filing fees on your client's behalf. On top of THOSE, there are the unexpected costs like the $500 brake job or the thousand-dollar medical bill. When I calculated my first-year expenses, estimates showed that my all-in costs would be $50,000–$75,000. These are big, scary, serious numbers. But better to go in prepared—and have a well considered budget—than to find out four months into your practice that you must decide between spending $500 on your mortgage or your office rent, or sending it to the district court because you have to cover the filing fees for that last minute counter-complaint.

### Q: What are some of the satisfactions of having your own law practice?

**A:** It's great having the freedom to set my own schedule. The downside is that I start to set my schedule for the convenience of my clients by opening early, staying late, or having weekend hours. It's great for clients, but it cuts into time with my family. I know there is a solution, but I feel guilty taking time off or even shorting my working hours; it feels a bit like I am abandoning my baby. The other thing about a solo's autonomy is that I have the office space to myself; I can bring my dogs and/or parrot into work, I can turn up the volume on my favorite music, and I can wander the halls muttering without worrying that someone will be concerned for my sanity. The downside is that there's no one to have lunch with (the dogs aren't big on conversation).

### Q: And the frustrations …?

**A:** [If you haven't heard], solo practitioners are the red-headed stepchildren of the legal profession. And the consensus is that if we were really good lawyers, we'd be working for one big firm or another. My frustration is with this persistent, subtle hostility, especially when I hear that how I choose to practice law (collaborative family), how I choose to bill my clients (mostly fixed fees, a little hourly), and that I chose to solo right out of law school, is backwards, wrong, silly; perhaps even bordering on malpractice. The one bright spot is that, occasionally, I talk with a lawyer (usually a solo/small) who gets what I'm trying to do and why I'm trying to do it, and gives me heartfelt wishes for success. Beyond that, most of my daily frustrations are those any business experiences; clients who pay late and vendors who deliver late. But these are transient frustrations, and can be corrected with the proper administration of chocolate, riding my horses, and—in extreme cases—Scotch.

## Q: What about job security?

**A:** When I was trying to decide if I should solo or not, the thought of having little to no job security scared the willies out of me and made for sleepless nights. Now that I am a solo, I come home so exhausted that sleeping is not a problem. Seriously, the lack of job security is worrisome, but that's just one of the trade-offs you make. It's all how you approach it; either you fret and worry about [the lack of job security], or it becomes the impetus to start marketing and building your practice.

## Q: What sort of business plan do you need?

**A:** It doesn't have to be fancy or follow any formal outline; nor does it be more than a set of bullet points. All it needs to do is outline what you are going to do, with whom you are going to do it, and how you are going to do it. But don't just write it and put it away. Refer to it regularly, and update it when necessary. But stay focused on your original purpose. Without a road map, you won't know how to get there…or know when you've arrived.

## Q: Does a new solo need malpractice insurance?

**A:** Check with your local bar; it may be a requirement. If it's not, get it anyway. It helps you sleep at night. Besides, most malpractice insurance providers are good for a free ethics CLE or two and they are usually quite willing to help you design good workable practice management solutions that can help reduce your premium. The only problem with malpractice insurance is figuring out how much coverage is needed. My provider told me to imagine what an average claim might be and get enough coverage to cover two claims per year. In the end, I chose the most coverage I could afford.

## Q: What advice do you have for new solos

**A:** Have a mentor or two. Don't try to spread yourself across multiple practice areas. Focus on one and become competent in that field before adding additional practice areas. Attend all the CLE's in your practice area that you can afford. Not only are they a great way to learn the in's and out's of your practice area, they are a great place to find mentors and to network. Have faith in yourself. If you weren't competent to practice law, the Court would not have granted you your license. Don't rush out and get that subscription to Westlaw or Lexis. Learn to use the free research services out there.

### Q: What's the future for solo practitioners?

**A:** [In my opinion], the practice of law is swinging towards an era of solo and small firm practices because of their flexibility and ability to innovate. It will be the solo/smalls who evolve their practices to fill niches as they become available, and to respond to the ebb & flow of the practice of law. We are facing a period of time where we have a glut of lawyers. My guess is that most of the attrition will come from those firms would fund their operation by borrowing on their accounts receivable, followed closely by those who maintain rigid adherence to the billable hour fee model. This may not be an extinction event, but you can see it from here.

### Q: Given what you've learned, would you still solo?

**A:** I will always have doubts about my decision to go solo, but in the final analysis it has been a fantastic learning experience. Whether or not I succeed as a solo, I am glad to be traveling this path.

Excerpted from Solo by Choice, The Companion Guide: 34 Questions That Could Transform Your Legal Career (Carolyn Elefant, 2011)

# APPENDIX 2

# Outtakes from Rurallawyer.com

*Rurallawyer.com,* twice named among Minnesota's Top 25 legal blogs, is author Bruce Cameron's blog about practicing law in rural America, out beyond the availability of broadband Internet and past the suburban sprawl, where good neighbors are a mile down the road, where the next lawyer is two towns over, and where the nearest Starbucks is a good hour away. What follows are five sample blogposts:

## Sample post #1

Perhaps the reason I am a rural lawyer is simply that friends and neighbors asked. It is a fact of small town life that gossip travels faster than the Internet, so it was not surprising that soon after I was accepted to law school my neighbors began asking me what I was going to do after law school. Naturally I would expound on my future plans much to the dismay of my questioner (if their rapidly dulling eyes were any indicator). Once I had finished and my questioner had regained the power of thought, their ending comment was invariably, *"Well y'know, there hasn't been a lawyer in town since ol' Bob Smith retired in the 60's. We sure could use one"*. Then again, the reason could be the current economic realities. When law jobs are scarce, it is often easier to create your own job than try to fish in a drying pool. So, perhaps I became a rural lawyer by default. It was far easier to create a practice close to home than 20 miles and 30 minutes away. It leads to a better work-life balance. So, I guess that I'm a rural lawyer because it fits me, because I fell into it, because I was asked to, because I feel a sense of purpose, and because… just because.

## Sample post #2

A fundamental difference between a small town and a small city is that small towns, regardless of their population, still have courthouses whereas small cities, in their hurry to morph into bedroom communities for some urbane metropolis, have justice centers. Justice centers are grand buildings, integrating glass, steel, and stone into a monument to bureaucratic judicial efficiency, providing one-stop shopping for all things legal from the sheriff to the recorder and from the courtroom to the jail cell. These are places [where] a cold sterility seems to make courtesy appear artificial, and it channels the mass of humanity that enters its walls into tired, well-worn roles. Courthouses, on the other hand, are quiet buildings sitting in silent dignity on the edge of the town square; more cathedral than monument. [They] were built out of pride and are maintained out of tradition. There is warmth within those weathered walls that encourages courtesy—more as an act of devotion than a gentile gesture—and welcomes those who enter. Recently I've had similar matters in both a small city justice center and a small town courthouse. In the former, the matter was concluded in a matter 10 minutes; a business transaction handled in the crisp efficiency only a streamlined & work-flowed process can provide. In the Courthouse, the matter took about twice as long, but, along the way, I got caught up on what's new in town, the weather, and the health of a friend's dog. Both matters were billed as fixed fees, but only one made me glad to have put on my lawyer suit that day.

**Sample post #3**

That the good ol' boy network is alive and well in rural communities should be no surprise to anyone. Nor should it surprise anyone that breaking into that network is hard for outsiders (that is, anyone whose family has not lived in the community for fewer than three generations). [But if you're willing], there are a few ground rules one must know before the doors of any one particular network will begin to crack open. Be polite, be very polite. This is beyond the common courtesies of please and thank you. This is about addressing people you don't know well as Mr., Mrs., or Miss, about hand-written thank-you notes, about using sir or ma'am when addressing your elders, or those who hold some position of authority. Regardless of how modern the town is in terms of infrastructure, you'll find that the attitudes and social expectations are much more Leave It to Beaver then The Simpsons. Be competent and honor your word. Small communities expect and respect competence—to be known as "someone who'll do right by you" is a high accolade—and most small communities still operate on a handshake. Nothing will cut you out of the ol' boy network faster than a reputation of failing to live up to your word. Be a follower before being a leader. You are the novice in this game and don't know the "whys" behind the way things are done. So, don't automatically assume that your "new" or "better" is actually an improvement. Take the time to pay your dues; these networks are built on trust and it is hard to trust the unknown. And don't assume that the ol' boy network is limited to boys. The ol' boys recognize that competence crosses gender lines.

## Sample post #4

The Atlanta Journal-Constitution recently reported that there exists a dearth of lawyers in rural Georgia. It seems the problem is not a numbers issues; after all, there are some 28,000+ lawyers in Georgia. The problem is one of distribution. Nearly 70 percent of the Georgia Bar practices within the five counties surrounding Metro Atlanta, leaving just under 9,000 lawyers spread across the remaining 154 counties, 35 of which have fewer than four practicing attorneys! The recurring theme of this blog is that rural lawyers are a vanishing species. This is a bad thing if you happen to live in a small town and need a lawyer; it is a good thing if you're the only attorney for within 150 miles. But [based on personal experience], I can tell you that starting a rural practice is not just a matter of showing up. It takes time for you and your small town to connect, and, until you get over being the New Kid in Town, income from your practice is going to be a bit lean. As the rural bar is starting a fast descent towards extinction, state Bar Associations and law schools are beginning to take note. The South Dakota Bar has created a task force to help connect lawyers to small towns, and the Iowa Bar is looking into loan forgiveness programs as well as programs to improve job placement for lawyer's spouses as ways to attract and keep small town lawyers. Both the University of Nebraska College of Law and the North Dakota School of Law are developing coursework and mentoring programs targeted toward developing rural solo/small practice lawyers. So, for the lawyer willing to take a chance on a less traveled career path, help is out there.

## Sample post #5

So, what does a state do when 65% of the state's lawyers practice in 4 of the 66 counties and 19 counties have 2 or fewer practicing lawyers. Well, if you are the South Dakota Senate, you float a plan to subsidize law student tuition in return for a promise that these students will open a practice in a small town or rural county. It's a cool idea—the county in need ponies up 1/3 of the student's school fees, the state's Unified Judicial System covers the remainder and the student contracts to keep their grades up and upon graduating to live and practice in the supporting county for a set number of years—and, a good start to reversing the declining rural lawyer population—let's hope it passes. But realistically, this is just a first step (a good one, but a first one).

It will take more than simply releasing a few dozen newly fledged lawyers out into the wild. If these future rural lawyers are to have a fighting chance to develop a thriving practice, they'll need more than a debt-free education; these new lawyers are going to need mentors, help with the administrative side of things, and a good education in keeping their overhead low. I'm betting the SD Bar has some ideas on how to solve these problems as well.

APPENDIX 3

# A New Practice Checklist

## 1. Before You Hang Your Shingle
- Develop a business plan (see Chapter 18, page 81)
- Write your vision statement
- Write your target market statement
- Write your core values statement
- Write your core services statement
- Develop a budget that factors in estimated living expenses, rent, transportation, personnel, insurance, bar dues & license fees, and loans from bank, family, friends, credit cards, etc.)
- Research your need for equipment, supplies, software (see Chapter 21), and CLE's.

## 2. Before You Open the Doors
- You need insurance, including commercial property & general liability, fire & theft for replacement value, file replacement & valuable papers coverage, umbrella coverage (if possible), professional liability (occurrence if at all possible), health, disability & life, workers compensation & employer liability, non-owned automobile coverage. Note: ask your State Bar if it has group insurance policies or if it sponsors a mutual insurance company that offers discounts to members).
- Get your federal and state EIN's.
- Get state & city permits if necessary
- As required by your state, send your contact information to the State Bar, Professional Responsibility Board, etc.
- Open your bank accounts (Business and IOLTA (trust) accounts). Be sure to order checks.
- Get a safe deposit box
- Arrange a line of credit and overdraft protection

- Get a domain name and e-mail address
- Setup a Web site for your firm
- Join community organizations (the local Bar, local chamber of commerce)
- Get on the list for court-appointed work
- Set your initial fees and fee structure
- Develop contacts with mentors and advisors. Know where to go for assistance.

### 3. Some Office Considerations

- Do you prefer space in an office suite that shares a conference room, waiting area, and receptionist? If so, you'll need just a simple private office of 150 to 200 square feet. Note: shared office suites usually aren't available in the smallest of small towns, but they can be found in moderately sized communities.
- Do you prefer a stand-alone office? You'll probably need some 400 to 600 sq. ft. (including 150 to 200 sq. ft. to meet clients, 150 to 200 sq. ft. for an assistant, and 100 to 200 sq. ft. for a reception area and storage). You save money if you can do without windows; interior offices often rent at a significant discount.
- When scouting locations, consider whether the office will be easy for clients to find, whether the office has a good layout, and whether it is close to some place to eat? Also, will the office have separate controls for heating and cooling, and that the electrical outlets and phone jacks are where you need them?
- What about signage?
- Lease considerations:

  Is parking for you and your staff included?
  Is there night and weekend access?
  Are furnishings supplied?
  Are utilities included?
  Is carpet cleaning and repainting included?
  Does the office have janitorial service, security services?

  **Tip:** When comparing rents, always compare the net square footage cost (e.g., the area of the office you can walk on; gross square footage is the total within the outer walls). There can be up to a 20 percent difference in area between the two measurements. Also, you'll need to know if the rent includes Common Area Maintenance (CAM), or any other common expenses and services (utilities, repairs, insurance and taxes). And don't forget to get everything in writing.

## 4. Some Office Equipment Basics

- You'll need a computer, monitor, and external disk drive for you and an assistant.
- You'll need a desk, desk chair, and floor pad for you and an assistant. Note: used furniture of higher quality usually lasts longer and often is less expensive than what find in discount furniture stores. You'll also need tables for your computers and printers; bookshelves; reading lamp; coat rack; reception-area furniture; at least four visitor chairs; office supplies and paper supplies (stationery, business cards, envelopes, Post-Its™, legal pads, note pads, etc.).
- You'll need telephone(s), a router, printer, scanner/copier, office software, word processor, contact/calendar/e-mail system, accounting software, a practice management system, and a system to back up your files.

  **Tip #1:** ask vendors and suppliers if discounts are available for early payment. In fact, always ask your suppliers for discounts. If such discounts are not available, pay your bills as late as possible while still avoiding penalties. The longer you keep your money, the longer it is working for you.

  **Tip #2:** buying printer ink and toner cartridges in bulk and using recycled cartridges can save up to 50 percent on the cost of these supplies compared to buying new.

  **Tip #3:** don't get carried away with custom logos, engraved letterhead, and embossed business cards, etc. Computer-printed letterhead on plain, good-quality envelopes saves money, as will one-color business cards.

  **Tip #4:** Buying refurbished equipment can get you this year's hot models at a significant savings. Generally, the price difference between new and refurbished is enough to cover the cost of an extended warranty and still yield a slight savings. If you're in the market for refurbished equipment, selection varies from day to day so be prepared to buy when you see the equipment you want.

## 5. As You Open Your Doors

- Develop your paper-handling and client file systems.
- Determine how to handle mail, deliveries, faxes, and messages.
- Determine how you will provide receipts and logs for incoming and outgoing monies, client documents, and client property
- Develop naming conventions for files and documents

*Client matters*
- Conflict of Interest checks
- Client files: Indexed or a database? Most likely this will be determined by your practice management system.

*Client relations*
- Standard letters for engagement, non-engagement, withdrawal & termination. Be sure you communicate your fees and your deadlines to clients.
- Develop a phone call/e-mail return policy
- Develop policies for file retention and copies to clients.

*Time management*
- Dual or single calendar system?
- Tickler system?
- Deadline management?
- Timekeeping?

*Critical tasks*
- Case/Matter planning.
- Practice development.
- Practice administration.
- Bookkeeping and accounting.

*Opening your practice*
- Announce your practice.
- Send announcements to the local bar, existing clients, to friends and family, to professional and social organizations you belong to, etc. Tweet about it, blog about it, put it up on your Facebook page.
- Submit a press release to the local press.
- Host an open house

  **Tips:**
  Don't buy what you can borrow,
  Don't buy until you have exhausted the free resources provided by your state bar association,
  Don't buy until you have exhausted the free online resources,
  Don't buy new if you can buy used,
  Don't invest in a subscription with a legal search provider until you have to, and
  Only invest in the resources you need for your major practice area(s).

# APPENDIX 4
# Bibliography

## Small Town Living
*50 Best Small Southern Towns* (Sweitzer & Fields, 2007)
*Best Places to Raise Your Family* (Sperling, 2006)
*Escape to a Small Town* (Rogak, 1999)
*Habits of the Heartland* (MacGregor, 2010)
*Making Your Move to One of America's Best Small Towns* (Crampton, 2002)
*Moving to a Small Town* (Urbanska & Levering, 1996)
*Moving to Small Town America* (Seavey, 1996)
*National Geographic's Guide to Small Town Escapes* (2000)
*Small Firms, Big Opportunity* (Hanson & Williams, 2012)
*Small Town Bound* (Clayton, 2001)
*The 100 Best Small Towns in America* (Crampton, 1996)
*The New Rating Guide to Life in America's Small Cities* (Heubusch, 1997)

## Practice Management
*How to Start and Build a Law Practice* (Foonberg, 2004)
*Social Media for Lawyers* (Elefant, Black, 2010)
*Solo by Choice* (Elefant, 2nd ed., 2011)
*The Curmudgeon's Guide to Practicing Law* (Hermann, 2006)
*The Freelance Lawyering Manual* (Alderman, 2011)
*Time Management for Attorneys* (Powers & McNalis, 2008)

## Entrepreneurship and Marketing
The Innovator's Solution (Christensen & Raynor, 2003)
*Permission Marketing* (Godin, 2002)
*The Big Red Fez: How to Make Any Web Site Better* (Godin, 2002)
*Guerrilla Marketing* (Levinson, 4th ed., 2007)
*How Good Attorneys Become Great Rainmakers* (Powers & McNalis, 2009)
*Social Media Marketing For Dummies* (Zimmerman & Sahlin, 2010)

**Client Experience**

*Clued In: How to Keep Customers Coming Back Again and Again* (Carbone, 2004)

*Good to Great* (Collins, 2001)

*Unleashing the Ideavirus* (Godin, 2001)

# APPENDIX 5

# Print & Online Resources

## Business Plans, Business Development, and Marketing

*Ten Questions For Lawyers To Ask Themselves When They Are Considering Starting Their Own Practices* (expertlaw.com/library/practice_management/starting_practice.html)

*Questions That Must Be Asked When Forming a Firm* (msba.org/departments/commpubl/publications/bar_bult/2003/april03/solo.htm)

*Getting Started* (okbar.org/members/map/CallowayGettingStarted.pdf)

*All Your Eggs in One Basket: Boutique Law Practice* (abanet.org/genpractice/magazine/2005/jul-aug/eggs.html)

*Naming Law Firms* (nonbillablehour.com/2004/02/naming_law_firm.html)

*Programs and Services to Help You Start, Grow and Succeed* (sba.gov/smallbusinessplanner/index.html)

*The Marketing Mind* (practicesmarter.com/2010/02/25/the-marketing-mind)

*How to Write Your Own Marketing Plan*
msba.org/departments/loma/articles/marketing/writemktgplan.htm

## Implementing and Monitoring Your Marketing Plan

*Law Firm Marketing Action Steps to Identify Your Ideal Target Audience* (articlesbase.com/marketing-articles/law-firm-marketing-action-steps-to-identify-your- ideal-target-audience-569282.html)

*The Complete Start-Up Guide* (abacuslaw.com/startup/TheCompleteStartupGuide.pdf)

*Start-up Kit for a Small Law Practice* (texasbarcle.com/materials/special/lawpractice.pdf)

*Tom Kane's Legal Marketing Blog* (legalmarketingblog.com/)

*Carolyn Elefant's My Shingle* (myshingle.com)

### Leases

*Leasing Office Space*
 (thestartuplawyer.com/startup-issues/leasing-office-space)

*Five Things to Consider Before Leasing Office Space*
 (officelease.com/pubs/2375_001.pdf)

### Insurance

*Checklist for Purchasers of Malpractice Insurance.*
 (abanet.org/legalservices/lpl/downloads/checklist.pdf)

*How to Prevent Gaps in Your Malpractice Coverage*
 (abanet.org/legalservices/lpl/downloads/preventinggaps.pdf)

### Fees

*A Financial Checklist for the New Solo Firm.*
 (abanet.org/lpm/magazine/articles/v33/is1/an18.shtml)

*Are You Charging What You're Worth?*
 (practicesmarter.com/2010/02/08/are-you-charging-what-youre-worth)

*The New Rules of Law Firm Profitability*
 (abanet.org/lpm/lpt/articles/fin08081.shtml)

*Flat Fees and Contingency Fees; Do They Fix Hourly Rates?*
 (abanet.org/lpm/lpt/articles/fin06071.shtml)

*Two Techniques to Dramatically Improve a Law Firm's Net Profit*
 (abanet.org/lpm/lpt/articles/fin04081.shtml)

*What Do Solo and Small Firm Lawyers Earn?* (myshingle.com/2010/03/articles/solo-practice-trends/what-do-solo-and-small-firm-lawyers-earn-2)

### Office Efficiency, Standardization, and Procedures

*A Rose by Any Other Name: Characteristics of an Efficient Practice*
 (abanet.org/lpm/lpt/articles/fin05041.html)

*The Importance of Systematizing Your Firm* (Practicesmarter.com/2010/04/12/the-importance-of-systematizing-your-firm)

*Purge Piles of Paper Pronto*
 (Practicesmarter.com/2009/10/29/purge-piles-of-paper-pronto)

*Email Etiquette for Lawyers* (Practicesmarter.com/2010/03/18/judge-writes-about-email-etiquette-for-lawyers/)

*Keep Your Inbox Under Control* (Practicesmarter.com/2010/03/08/keep-your-inbox-under-control/)

## Bar Associations

*Are You a Bar Association Member?* (Practicesmarter.com/2009/11/23/are-you-a-bar-association-member)

*Raising the Bar: Get the Most Out of Your Bar Association* (abanet.org/tech/ltrc/publications/loc_barwebsites200212.html)

## Rural Resources

*American Mobility: Who Moves? Who Stays Put? Where's Home?* (Taylor, Morin, Cohn, Wang; Pew Research Center, Dec. 29, 2008)

*Internet, Broadband, and Cell Phone Statistics* (Rainie, Pew Research Center, Jan. 5, 2010)

*The Return of the Multi-Generational Family Household* (Taylor, Pew Research Center, March 18, 2010)

*Take This Job and Love It* (Morin, Pew Research Center, Sept.17, 2009)

*Federal Communications Commission, Internet Access Services: Status as of December 31, 2009* (Industry Analysis and Technology Division Wireline Competition Bureau December 2010)

*A Comparison of Rural and Urban Legal Experience* (Landon, Great Plains Research: A Journal of Natural and Social Sciences, 2(1), 1992, pp 67–96)

The Growth Potential of Small Town Law (Furlong, The Lawyers Weekly, Dec. 3, 2010, lawyersweekly.ca/index.php?section=article&volume=30&number=29&article=5)

*Demographic Trends in Rural and Small Town America* (Johnson, Carsey Institute, Vol 1(1), 2006)

*America's Wealthiest (and Poorest) States* (Christie, CNNMoney.com, Sept.16, 2010, money.cnn.com/2010/09/16/news/economy/Americas_wealthiest_states/index.htm

*Rural Pro Bono Delivery* (americanbar.org/content/dam/aba/migrated/2011_build/probono_public_service/aba_rural_book_2011.authcheckdam.pdf)

*How Portable Is Your Life?* (Korkki, New York Times, Nov. 7, 2010, pp BU14. nytimes.com/2010/11/07/jobs/07search.html?_r=2&emc=eta1&)

# APPENDIX 6

## Footnotes

### Chapter 1

1. *Demographic Trends in Rural and Small Town America* (Johnson, Carsey Institute, Vol 1(1), 2006)
2. The term "micropolitan" was coined by the US Census Bureau to designate a rural area that contains at least one urban place with a population of at least 10,000.

### Chapter 3

1. *American Mobility: Who Moves? Who Stays Put? Where's Home?* (Taylor, Morin, Cohn, Wang; Pew Research Center, Dec. 29, 2008)
2. *Moving to Small Town America: How to Find & Fund the Home of Your Dreams* (Seavey, 1996)
3. Lark Toys, Kellogg Minnesota
4. *Moving to Small Town America: How to Find & Fund the Home of Your Dreams* (Seavey, 1996)
5. Ibid, page 173

### Chapter 9

1. *A Lawyer's Story: Returning Home* (Penfield, 2012); http://reimaginerural.com/a-lawyers-story-returning-home
2. *Green Acres*, by Leslie A. Gordon (ABA Journal, Nov. 2009)

### Chapter 13

1. I first learned of this technique from Steven Yasgur, a Collaborative lawyer practicing in Edina, MN

## Chapter 17
1. *Clued In: How to Keep Customers Coming Back Again and Again* (Carbone, 2004)
2. *Guerrilla Marketing* (Levinson, 4th ed., 2007)

## Chapter 20
1. The Cost of Data Loss, David M. Smith (Graziado Business Review, Vol. 6 Issue 3, 2006)
2. Boston Computing Network, Data Loss Statistics (www.bostoncomputing.net/consultation/databackup/statistics/)

Made in the USA
Middletown, DE
25 January 2015